Mobilität und Normenwandel

Changing Norms and Mobility

Band **17** Volume

Herausgegeben von
edited by

Rüdiger Voigt

in Verbindung mit
in connection with

Rainer S. Elkar, Jürgen Reulecke und Jürgen Zinnecker

1996

Mobilität und
Normenwandel

Changing Norms
and Mobility

As-C-IV-111

———————— Band **17** Volume ————————

Israel

A Contemporary
Political Geography

by
Elisha Efrat

Universitätsverlag Dr. N. Brockmeyer
1996

Die Reihe MOBILITÄT UND NORMENWANDEL - CHANGING NORMS AND MOBILITY erscheint in zwangloser Folge.

Herausgeber ist Professor Dr. jur. Rüdiger Voigt, Vorstand des Instituts für Staats-wissenschaften, Fakultät für Sozialwissenschaften, Universität der Bundeswehr München, D-85577 Neubiberg, Tel. 0 89 / 60 04-23 80 / 23 76, Fax 0 89 / 60 04-30 59.

ISSN 0179-7883
ISBN 3-8196-0455-3
Alle Rechte vorbehalten
© 1996 by Universitätsverlag Dr. N. Brockmeyer
Uni-Tech-Center, Gebäude MC, 44799 Bochum
Gesamtherstellung: Druck Thiebes GmbH Hagen
Gedruckt auf chlorfrei gebleichtem Papier

Die Deutsche Bibliothek – CIP-Einheitsaufnahme

Efrat, Elisha:
Israel – a contemporary political geography / by Elisha Efrat. –
Bochum : Brockmeyer, 1996
   (Mobilität und Normenwandel ; Bd. 17)
   ISBN 3-8196-0455-3

NE: GT

Contents

Preface

This book, dealing with contemporary geography and politics of Israel, is an attempt to analyze current political events against the background of the geographical space in which they took place, and is based on a follow–up, record and study of the main events that occurred in the two last decades and their impact on Israel's future towards the 21st century.

Since the Six Day War in 1967, the geography of Israel has changed radically, mainly in subjects as the political borderlines, the new layout of towns and villages, the distribution of population to new areas which were not under Israeli sovereignty, mass–immigration of Russian Jews, the increase of the Israeli Arab population, the growth of Jerusalem and the population increase in the central coastal plain around Tel Aviv, and the rapid increase of traffic, the rate of motorization and above all – negotiations with the Palestinians, and first steps towards a possible freedom with Israel's neighbouring states. It seems, that the decades after 1967 were the most intensive and dynamic ones Israel ever experienced, both in their amount of events and in their rapid occurrence.

Since the Six Day War most of the changes that happened took place beyond the official 'Green Line' borders including main geographical and political issues as: territory, settlement, rural and urban development, land use, housing, transportation and employment. These issues imprinted their influence on the new administered areas of Judea, Samaria, the Gaza Strip and the Golan Hights, created spatial and demographic changes, but with a flimsy connection to the social and economic fabric that exists within Israel. It seems, that although the tremendous investments that the government made in the territories, there is no big chance to dominate them in the future because of their demographic, social and ethnic complexity.

The outcome of the Six Day War and the activities of the Social Democratic and right–wing governments in the years 1977–1992 brought to the fore political and territorial matters that the State was compelled to deal with. The conquest of territory and its occupation; the settlement of areas across the borders for the purpose of controlling them or turning them into a bargaining card in peace negotiations; the emergence of Jewish national ties with the Greater Land of Israel movement; all of the massive investment in the physical infrastructure of the occupied areas to the detriment of development Israel within the so–called 'Green Line' that marked the boundary of Israel as determined by the Armistice Agreement of 1949, and certain political acts such as the creation of Greater Jerusalem, the annexation of the Golan Heights, the withdrawal from Sinai, and from most of the Gaza Strip, and later on from some of the big towns in Judea and Samaria – all these exemplify how geography and politics interact in the current period.

Despite the prominence of politics in Israel life, it has not been properly taken into account from the professional geographical point of view. A study of current political events against a spatial background, and all that this applies, has not so far been undertaken. There is no period as fitted as recent decades to facilitate a proper investigation, description and analysis of this aspect of politics.

The various chapters in this book treat subjects of great interest and importance for the life in Israel today, such as Jewish settlements and settlers in Judea and Samaria, the revival of the 'Green Line', the 'Intifada' as an Arab uprise, the urban political geography of Jerusalem, the future of the Golan Heights, Israel's water problems, the new development towns of Israel and the handling of the mass immigrations from different countries. These and many others have been analyzed and demonstrated, herewith, from a geographical and political standpoint.

Siegen 1995   **E. Efrat**

The Scope of Contemporary Political Geography

Significant contemporary geographical and political events can be described and analyzed within short spans of time since their occurrence, can be relied to the near past or with the existing present, which validate them an actual dimension. Such a dimension arises a basic question: what lies between actuality and contemporary geography? Actualism is a philosophical method which argues, that reality is not an object or a situation which exists permanently, but a procedure of uninterrupted activity. There exists in the world a certain order of facts and a perpetual flow of events. Therefore, actual facts should not be observed just as they appear, but in connection with the origin of their creation, which is the act, and then on – with their continuity till the present.

Even objects in a space exist in a perpetual dynamic change. Although geographical elements as mountains, valleys, seas, lakes and lands are often described as static objects, in reality they are not so, because they undergo changes, especially if additional factors have their influence upon them, as climate, water, population, settlements, communications etc. Therefore, geography, should not relate to a certain event as a monodimential or a static one, but as to a phenomenon which appears in a certain time and in a certain form, has a short or a long past, but always a future, within a continuing process of existence and fading. Moreever, geography should not describe and analyse a certain phenomenon or demonstrate an event only by its classical elements and accumulated knowledge based on the past. Such description or analysis, as far as being interesting, might be unuseful, because the geographical contemporary event includes mostly new elements, processes, relations and implications, which did not exist in the past. Events may appear in new relations and circumstances which might intertest the public much more than those described with historical and basic geographical elements.

As against the comprehensive and static conception in geography, time comes to relate geography with its elements and its ideas to actual and contemporary occurrences, to explain spatial events by their dynamic trends, to change classical emphasizes which were used in past descriptions, and to adopt a new conception in the frame of a so called "contemporary geography". People are used to percept phenomena and events in an inductive way, from partiality to generally. A concentration of many particularities with clear and common characteristics might lead them to a general way of thinking and to the understanding of a subject in its wide meaning. The deductive approach in geography, which tries to explain facts and events from the generally to to the particularly, was not always found to be effective to understand actual occurrences, because the mental transfer from generally to present reality does not always appear successively, because it is connected with a change in proportion and scale of events, and therefore not easily conceived. It is worthwile to develop an inductive approach in geography, which relates to detailed facts ond occurrences as a point of departure to the understanding of the generally, and after screening of details, to try to explain the more wider ties that exist between the facts. The basic aim in contemporary geography is therefore to analyze a certain event with all its components, to isolate it in order to describe and understand its elements and their dynamic development, to explain it on a general physical, human, economic, social and regional background, and then to draw conclusions from the reasons of its formation to its future occurrences. The conclusions which could be drawn from these relationships from a geographical event might be practicable and executable, for instance, by demonstrating a political standpoint, by sounding an alarm against danger, or by the need to take a preventive step against it. When such conclusions exist, results may be conveyed to bodies or agencies that have the power to change facts.

By contemporary geography, which concentrates in facts of the present, in their reality and in the background of their creation, there is no intention to establish a new field in geography in addition to those which already exist, as settlement, rural, urban, political or climatical geography, but to propose a meaningful change in the approach, which should project its applied and practical aspects in every field it is involved in, and to analyze contemporary events by their spatial components. By this approach the need to emphasize the actual element in geography should be perpetual and selective. Perpetual in order to react to the sequence of events in a professional way, and not as a single act, and selective - in order to handle those meaningful events in which geography has the capacity to contribute its knowledge. The aim of such a contemporary approach is to make the geographical discipline more popular for the public and more clear, while demonstrating its vitality in handling actual problems, and to make its value equal to physical, social and human sciences.

It seems, that geography as against actualism finds itself sometimes in a quite complexive position. On one hand, geography deals with enormous information on the whole world, has specific tools in cartography which no other science owns, has tools and methods for general analysis and integrative perspectives of phenomena, and is almost the only science which is able to analyze and to explain space with most of its components. On other hand, geography does not utilize actually enough its global knowledge to relate to contemporary events. One may get the impression that geography is threathened by some kind of a psychological and methodological barrier which prevents it to react professionally and be involved in space problems.

As against the lack of actual consequences in many of the geographical researches which have been carried out in Israel in the past, more steps are taken nowadays to challenge with actual problems, and to deal with concrete events that have spatial importance, and to draw from them the operational conclusions. Such a trend mainly appears in subjects which relate to political and social sciences. Nevertheless, geography has the power to withstand many actual problems which need solutions, or at least provide a special academic approach to them from a spatial point of view.

In order to make Israel's geography vital and more useful and understandable by the public it increases its involvement in contemporary events. By that it is actual and gains prestige, and is more easily accepted by the media and will be developed as a contributing and influencing profession. Israelis have realized that so long geographical research will not lead to specific solutions of contemporary political and future problems, and its consequences and occurrences, it might reuce the importance of their discipline.

Israel's Political Map after the Six Day War

The settlement map of Israel today is very different from what it was in the 1950s and 1960s, and is continually being further altered by the development of additional new settlements throughout the area, by the internal migration of population to them, and by new priorities of political development. No other period in the history of the State of Israel has witnessed such rapid and significant changes in the settlement map. The decade of the 1970s was especially crucial, for it was then that Israel's ties were strengthened with the occupied territories beyond its political borders the Golan Heights, Judea and Samaria and the Gaza Strip, and for a shorter period – the Sinai Peninsula. A new map was drawn during that decade, influenced by the new political situation resulting from the Six Day War (1967). Israel then gained control of territories of different economic, social and demographic character, which for political and security reasons dictated a new settlement endeavour beyond its 1967 borders (Efrat, 1988).

The sovereign territory of Israel as established by the 1949 Armistice Agreement amounted 20,700 square kilometers. The zones occupied by Israel after the Six Day War added a periphery of 68,589 square kilometers, which was 3.3 times the area of Israel proper. Israel's territorial extension through the newly occupied territories could be summarized as follows: the Sinai peninsula - 61,198 square kilometers with very few rural and urban points, and no sovereignty over the area; the Golan Heights - 1,150 square kilometers - with planning and implementation of regional settlement throughout the entire area, establishment of a new town and more than 30 new settlements, with Israeli law applied to the region in 1981; Judea and Samaria - 5,878 square kilometers - with comprehensive, intensive rural and urban settlement against the background of a dense Arab settlement configuration, and without sovereignty over the area; and the Gaza Strip - 363 square kilometers - with limited Jewish settlement in the Qatif Bloc at its southern part, against a background of a dense Arab population, here too without sovereignty (Fig. 1).

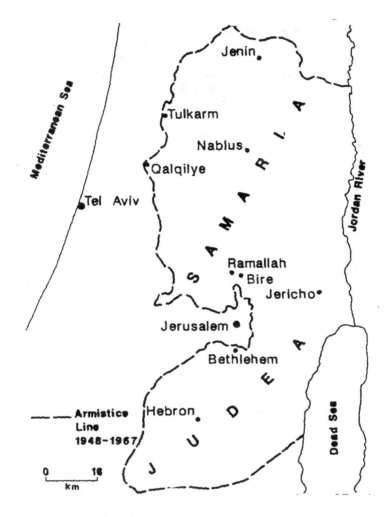

Fig. 1: The Occupied Territories after the Six Day War 1967

From north to south, Israel was 409 kilometers long before the Six Day War and 650 kilometers before the withdrawal from Sinai. Before 1967 there were 2,750,000 people in Israel with many areas sparsely populated, while in 1995 there were more than a 5.3

14

million on a territory just a third larger, with a distribution no better than the earlier one, and with 1.7 million Arabs in Judea, Samaria and the Gaza Strip. Israel recognized unilateral the Jordan River as the eastern border, the unilateral conversion of the Golan Heights armistice line into a political border, and the creation of a de–facto border between Israel and Lebanon along a narrow security zone beyond the recognized international border between the two countries.

Settlement and Development after 1967

Israel's new geopolitical goals after 1967 were the occupation, as rapidly as possible, of areas beyond the 'Green Line' by the establishment of numerous settlements; the creation of new security belts beyond the 1967 borders; continued socio–economic consolidation of previously established settlements within these borders; and further expansion of the infrastructure.

The ways in which these were to be achieved were basically the same as twenty years before. In this period too, border settlements were founded, although the borders were now in the Golan Heights, the Jordan Rift Valley and the north–east of the Sinai Peninsula. Development districts were set up on the Golan Heights, in the southern Gaza Strip, in the Jordan Valley, and at selected and more restricted spots.

Most of the development took place not within the sovereign domain of Israel, but far beyond it. This new development did not form a continuum with the settlement complexes established during the two previous decades. Moreover, the change in the priority in basic investments and the diversion of resources to the occupied territories left insufficient funds for the socio–economic consolidation of the settlements established in the past. In the 1970s a new settlement geography began to take shape, with comprehensive political and security interests beyond the original borderline. Development priority has also been accorded to Jerusalem throughout the years, despite the 33 development towns founded when the State was established to attract urban settlers and scatter the population. The desire was to transform the city into a large capital, for nationalist and religious reasons, although this was not justified on objective geographical grounds.

Instead of solving substansive and physical problems within the territory of Israel, accelerated development activity was being directed, as aid, to sites outside it. In the wake of the frustrations of the withdrawal from Sinai in 1981, and the enforced territorial shrinkage, the declared policy of the government gave greater impetus to the west-east direction, turning its attention to the occupied territories for reasons of security, strategic depth, and territorial integrity. The three objectives of this expansion were naturally the Golan Heights, the Gaza Strip, and Judea and Samaria. The Golan Heights had a great deal of unoccupied land and a small local population, while Judea and Samaria had both, considerable unoccupied land and a large population. On the Golan Heights the aquisition of physical control had been relatively easy and was already accomplished; in the Gaza Strip there was no possibility of expansion, because there were about 600 thousand people in an area of about 363 square kilometers, one of highest densities in the world. There thus remained one possible objective for expansion – Judea and Samaria.

It must be borne in mind that this latitudinal direction was beset with considerable difficulty, facing a million strong Arab population in dense concentrations throughout Judea and Samaria, facing a continuum of villages and towns, facing difficulties in acquiring land, and facing a hostile population that did not make things at all easy for the civil administration in the areas. The latitudinal expansion was based on a number of phenomena characteristic of the Israeli population. The Jewish population has a definitely urban mentality and is therefore prepared for non–agricultural settlement involving industry and services; it is interested in places of residence of improved environmental quality devoid of pollution; and it wishes to abandon disorderly urban crowding even for places beyond the 'Green Line'. The motivation derived from the fact that in Judea and Samaria it was possible to find relatively easy solutions to all the defects so glaring in Israel, and for which no reasonable solutions were planned in an exchanging territorial situations.

However, the authorities made a different response to the new geographical conditions. The changed direction they took disregarded the principles that had underline the upbuilding of the country in the past. There is no doubt that the settlement map of the 1970s and 1980s was influenced primarily by political, military and security factors, subject to pressure from the United States, Egypt and Syria which dictated various measures in Israel. Yet there were also various domestic nationalistic motives and political party interests that contributed to the settlement activities and the change in the map of Israel. In the course of the process, various social and economic pressure groups arose which were very much interested in having Israel change direction so that they could derive some benefit.

Thus the 1970s and the 1980s differ from all earlier decades in the emphasis on political motivations for settlement going beyond economic considerations, on massettlement rural and urban, public and private, in areas whose ultimate fate is not yet known, involving penetration of a crowded Arab fabric, on new types of settlement - and all this with a daily political struggle. Israel's new borders led to a reqrettable diffusion of the new settlements; it created too few consolidated areas as the Golan Heights and the Jordan Valley, and left some sparsely ones. In the past the Negev was chief focus of the settlement, later replaced by Galilee, and in the 1970s by Sinai, the Golan Heights, Judea and Samaria, and the Jerusalem environs. The right-wing Likud government fostered between 1977–1991 extreme politization in the settlement of Judea and Samaria, in order to change the map of the country within a short period of time and strengthen it toward the east. It is doubtful whether it is a map within which it will be possible to maintain uni-national sovereignty and a democratic society.

Changes of the 1990s Map

After signing the Oslo agreement between Israel and the Palestinians in 1993, an additional change occurred in the map of the occupied territories. Following the principle of conveying autonomy to the Palestinians in Judea, Samaria and the Gaza Strip, Israel decided to withdraw partially and stepwise from the territories, first from the Gaza Strip and the town of Jericho, and then from Six other cities, dependent on the advancement in the negotiations with the Palestinians. More than two–thirds of the Gaza Strip has been already returned to the Palestinians, as their autonomous region under Arafat's administration, and so Jericho as a Palestinian autonomous enclave in the Jordan Valley.

The geopolitical map of Israel might receive a further change in the near future with the proposed withdrawal of the Israelis from the big Arab towns in Judea and Samaria, as Jenin, Nablus, Tulkarm and Qalqilye, while the problematic town of Hebron with its 400 Jewish extreme fanatic Jewish people, will remain to the final stage of military evacuation. Certainly, the delicate and sensitive problem of Jerusalem is meanwhile not on the agenda of the bilateral negotiations, and will arise at the last stage of the peace treaty agreement with the Palestinians.

Geography and Policy in the Occupied Territories

In order to understand the geographical and political aspects in the occupied territories some relevant main historical periods and events in the Land of Israel should be demonstrated.

The term Judea and Samaria, or the West Bank, identifies a political and administrative unit comprising two areas of western Palestine that came under Jordanian rule between the Armistice Agreement of 1949 and the 1967 Six Day War. After 1949 these areas were deprived of their contacts with the adjacent coastal plain and outlets to the Mediterranean Sea. Their sole remaining land contacts were thus with the Hashemite Kingdom of Jordan. The Gaza Strip which is part of the Mediterranean coastal plain, 36 kilometers long but only 5-8 kilometers wide, and mostly covered by sand dunes, is an area which received political recognition in the 1949 Armistice Agreement between Israel and Egypt when it was made a seperate entity under the latter's supervision. Its contacts were since then with Egypt only.

Judea and Samaria lies on the central massif of Palestine, with Judea region in an average elevation of 1,000 meters, and Hebron as its main urban center, while Samaria region has an average elevation of 500 meter, with Nablus as its main center. Judea and Samaria together encompass 5,878 square kilometers. Between them lies Jerusalem, a mountainuos city under Israeli jurisdiction and functions as the regional center for both Judea and Samaria (Fig. 2).

Fig. 2: Judea and Samaria

The 1948 Arab–Israeli war led to a radical political economic change even in Jerusalem. In the Armistice Agreement of 1949 the city was divided into western and eastern sectors, the former under Israeli jurisdiction and the latter under Jordanian. The boundary between the two sections was the armistice line, or the 'Green Line'. Both parts developed different economic orientations, Israeli Jerusalem - to Tel Aviv and the coastal plain and East Jerusalem - to Amman and Trans-Jordan. So the result was - three different regions in their geography, delimited by artificial boundaries that divided politically, economically and culturally between two peoples, Jews and Arabs (Fig. 3).

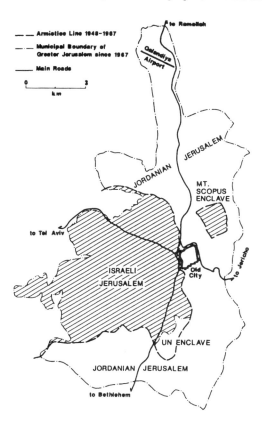

Fig. 3: Israeli and Jordanian Jerusalem 1948 - 1967

Judea, Samaria, the Gaza Strip and East Jerusalem together might be considered as insurgent regions. The Arab people who live there want a country of their own in a territory currently demonstrated by a government in which they have no participation. To advance their case, they engage in various activities, mainly terrorism and what was called by them 'Intifada'.

The Arab Population

The Arab population in Judea and Samaria is dispersed in 12 towns, most of them located on the mountains between Hebron in the south and Jenin in the north. In the west there lie the towns of Tulkarm and Qalqilye, and in the east Jericho. About 40% of the population is urban, while the rest lives in about 400 villages. In the Gaza Strip there are six towns, almost all of them grew from villages, except the capital of the region, the town of Gaza, which has a population of about 160,000 (Fig. 4).

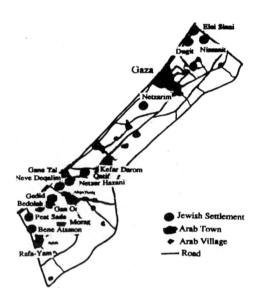

Fig. 4: Settlements in the Gaza Strip

There are more than a hundred thousand refugees dispersed in 20 camps in Judea and Samaria who left their towns and villages during the 1948-War. In the Gaza Strip refugees number approximately a quarter of a million, who live in eight camps. About one quarter of the Arab population in the territories reside in refugee camps. The camps are located near Arab towns and got the shape of squatter settlements. The camps have become an integral part of the landscape and permanent settlement for a population homogenous in origin, culture and circumstances. The camps arose on what once was vacant land near Arab towns along main traffic arteries. The quality of life in the camps has worsened over time. Few sources of employment have been created for the expanding population in or near the camps. The Israeli government contends that the refugees are an Arab problem, but the Arab countries see them as a Palestinian–Israel problem.

The Arab layout of towns and villages fits the geographical features of the area. Big towns along the mountainous crest connected by main roads, distribution of villages on fertile agricultural soil with no villages in the eastern semi-arid desert are typical to that region. In the Gaza Strip towns and villages fit the axis of a main historic road, the 'via maris', agricultural land and underground water resources.

Israel's conquest of Judea, Samaria, the Gaza Strip, Sinai peninsula, the Golan Heights and East Jerusalem in the 1967 War enabled to extend its frontiers, to improve its security and strategic position, and to realize what Jews perceive to be their historical rights to 'All the Land of Israel'. After the six Day War in 1967 the territories became under Israeli military administration and the previous orientation to orientation to Jordan has been partly replaced by linkages with Israel. During the conquest of Judea and Samaria some 250,000 Arabs fled the region. In the Gaza Strip most of the population remained, but was disconnected from Sinai and Egypt. Jerusalem became then a reunified city.

Demographic Factors

At the end of the Six Day War Judea and Samaria had approximately 595,000 inhabitants, some 225,000 of them in 12 urban centers. By 1995 the Arab population has increased to over a million. The rural population also intensed urbanization and is dispersed in more than 400 villages of various size. The main reason for the population expansion is the very high natural increase among the Arabs, approximately by 37 per thousand annually, in contrast with 19 per thousand for the Jews. The fecundity rate of Arab women is still 7 births per woman, while infant mortality is decreasing. The Arab population is much younger than the Jewish one. More then half of the Arabs in the occupied territories are less than five years old. This figure promises even higher population in the future. To that should be added the fact that the Arabs still live together in large families and that the attachment to their land does not encourage emigration.

In the Gaza Strip the demographics are even more striking. The population in 1995 totals approximately 800,000, with a density of more than 2,200 inhabitants per square kilometer, more than six times that of Israel and more than 10 times that of Judea and Samaria. The natural increase in the Gaza Strip is 47 per thousand annually, higher than in any other Arab country and one of the highest rates in the world. To illustrate the demographic situation it may be added that in 1995 there were about 1,050,000 Arabs in Judea and Samaria, 800,000 in the Gaza Strip and about 900,000 in Israel. In the occupied territories there live today about 1,850,000 Arabs against a population of 5.3 million in Israel, a proportion of 74:26. But by taking into account Israel's own 900,000 Arabs, we get that the proportion between Jews and Arabs in the whole Land of Israel is actually 4,300,000 Jews against 2,750,000 Arabs or 71:29. The Israel Central Bureau of Statistics has a forecast of 1,000,000–1,200,000 Arabs in Israel toward the year 2000, the same in the West Bank and a million in the Gaza Strip, all from natural increase.

As we see, demography plays against Israel, and although the country absorbs thousands of Jewish immigrants every year, it will never be able to overcome the natural increase of the Arab population. That might be a good argument for Israelis to seperate themselves from the territories in order to remain a real Jewish State.

Israel's Settlement Policy in the Territories

In July 1967 the government of Israel was presented by one of its ministers, Yigal Allon, with a plan for the future borders of the country, and which proposed principles concerning peace arrangements with neighbouring countries. This first political plan for Judea and Samaria applied mainly to the eastern part of Judea and Samaria and the Jordan Valley. Its value lay in the fact, that it was the first comprehensive attempt to formulate a clear territorial stand regarding Israel's most problematic border, that with Jordan. The boundaries of the plan, derived from topographic and demographic considerations, were set between two longitudinal axes, one along the Jordan river, and the other along the eastern slopes of the Samarian Mountains. Between these two there exists land suitable for cultivation and the area was rather sparsely populated. The approach regarding the Jordan Valley was based on a regional settlement concept of developmemt, with agricultural settlements aroud a regional center (Fig. 5).

22

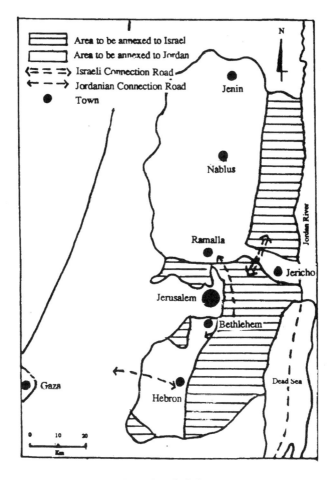

Fig. 5: The 'Allon' Plan

Allon viewed his plan as a peace plan, and therefore included the refugee problem among his assumptions. The plan was based on obtaining a territorial compromise which would meet Israel's security requirements and at the same time take into account the nationalistic aspirations of the Arab population in Judea, Samaria and Jordan. It proposed to include 40% of the area of Judea and Samaria under Israel sovereignty, following the conception of the Labour party which favoured the settlement of the

23

Jordan Valley as a security belt. The 'Allon Plan' was never formally approved by the Israeli government, but in the years after 1967 the governments acted in Judea and Samaria and the Gaza Strip in accordance with the principles of this plan. The Israeli governments of 1968-1977 approved settlements in areas beyond the 'Green Line' in accordance with the unofficial 'Allon Plan'. Settlement strategy under this plan was aimed at providing secure and defence along the eastern boundary of Israel.

The Settlement Policy

The Six Day War influenced significantly the settlement policy of Israel. The greatest changes occurred in places from which the Arabs fled. After the war various groups of people who believed in a hard line attitude to the Arab states and in the retention of all the newly incorporated territories, came to prominence in Israel's political life. The two major groups consisted of the right-wing Likud party and the religious nationalists of Gush Emunim were now the most prominent groups amongst the West Bank settlers. At the locational level, the new government gave a free hand to the activities to settle along the mountainous ridge in Judea and Samaria. This area, constituting the center of the Israelite Kingdoms, has not been settled by the previous Labour government since it did not constitute part of their policy of establishing defencible boundaries and also because this area contains the dense Arab population concentrations in the West Bank.

Quantitatively the process of settlement took the form of an exponential growth, with the year 1978 being the breaking point. It started as a return of Jewish inhabitants to their pre-1948 homes in settlements or neighborhoods evacuated in the 1948-War, as the Jewish Quarter in Old Jerusalem, the Etzyon Bloc and Hebron. Other more subtle forms followed later.

Jewish settlers in Judea and Samaria after 1967 confronted a population of 850,000 Arabs, who in course of time had occupied most of the sites for habitation. About 120 settlements, containing about 130,000 Jews, have been established in the region by the Israeli government till 1992. These Jewish settlements constitute three per cent of the Jewish population in Israel.

A similar policy has been implemented by Israel in the Gaza Strip. One example is the Qatif Bloc, an Israeli settlement zone in the southern part of the Gaza Strip. The Bloc was designed to act as a wedge seperating the Egyptian border of Sinai from the dense Arab population in the rest of the area, to maintain an Israeli presence in that sector of the occupied territories, and to establish a focus of Jewish settlement in a region whose political destiny was till then undetermined.

A most significant explication process was the post-1978 wave of settlement which implied the most spatio-economic potentialities of the West Bank, namely, its close proximity to the metropolitan region of Tel Aviv and the city of Jerusalem. The migration flows originated in four major regions. The Tel Aviv metropolitan area, the city of Jerusalem, Israel's periphery in the Galilee and in the Negev, and Jews from abroad. Nor migrants from Tel Aviv area moved to settlememts in West Samaria region, while most migrants from Jerusalem moved to a group of settlements around Jerusalem. The Haifa area contributed its part to the settlement in north Samaria, while the Israeli periphery contributed mostly to West Samaria or the Jerusalem area. Jewish colonization of the West Bank was mostly part of the metropolitan expansion of Tel Aviv and Jerusalem. The development eastwards started mainly after 1977 as a consequence of the massive and rapid construction of new settlements on the western fringes of the Samaria mountains. These settlements were constructed as suburbs, devoid of a local economic base, as part of a declared government policy, to attract the occupied territories. This was implemented by large-scale investments in land purchasing, the construction of infrastructure and housing projects, and by declaring the whole of the occupied territories as development area. This implied high government subsidies for housing and generous loans to private construction companies and to investion of industries.

The most prominent outcome of the Jewish settlement process in the occupied territories has been the reshaping of Israel's metropolitan fields. This has come out by expanding Tel Aviv Metropolitan zone of influence eastward into the occupied territories and by transforming Jerusalem from a medium-sized town before 1967 into a metropolis in 1995.

Many people in Israel suppose, that the Jewish settlement in the occupied territories is a way of no return. Although most of the settlements are not big, and include not more than 50-100 families each, their geographical location over all parts of the area enables them to dominate land and territory toward any political agreement or autonomy which may be accepted in the future. Also the enormous investments Israel has done in development, infrastructure and building in the region should be emphasized which might undermine a total withdrawal.

The Geographical–Political Situation of Jerusalem

The status and importance of the city throughout its long history has been determined by its location in a natural basin near the crest of the Judean hills, at the intersection of principal north-south and west-east routes. Since 1948 Jerusalem has usually been discussed in terms of a threefold division: the Old City, East Jerusalem and West Jerusalem. The Old City is conveniently and precisely defined by its impressive encircling walls built during the 16th century. East Jerusalem usually refers to the parts of the city outside the walls of the Old City that were under Jordanian rule between 1948-1967. Its population is mostly Arab. West Jerusalem has been under Israeli control since 1948 and the population is predominantly Jewish.

From 1948 to 1967 Jerusalem was a politically and a religiously divided city. The armistice line in 1949 confirmed the division of the city and created a neutral zone to be administered by the UN between the Jordanian and Israeli positions. The Jordanian army occupied the Old City and East Jerusalem, and the Israeli army controlled West Jerusalem. Most foreign governments did not transfer their embasis to Jerusalem. Nevertheless, Jerusalem has functioned as the 'de–facto' capital of Israel since 1950.

The population of the city was almost totally segregated on the basis of ethnicity: virtually no Arabs lived in West Jerusalem and no Jews inhabited East Jerusalem. The Jewish communities moved westward, while the Arab ones expanded eastward. The Arab sector of Jerusalem did not enjoy the level of organization and efficiency that characterized the Israeli portion. Part of the situation was the confused political circumstances that marked the fate of the Arab Palestinian territory which did not materialize, so that the Arab zone was absorbed by Jordan.

Shortly after the 1967-War Israel's annexation of East Jerusalem and the Old City brought Jerusalem under a single political control. The first task with symbolic and political significance was the reconstruction of the Jewish quarter in the Old City. A second objective involved the occupation of Mount Scopus with the Hebrew University, a symbol of renaissanse for Jews. The third objective was to establish Jewish neighbourhoods around the city that should dense settlement and discourage of any further armistice line. The fourth objective was to provide defensive barriers by extending the outer limit of new settlement to high ground around the city. The final objective was to make Jerusalem accessive from all directions.

Jerusalem is a microcosm of the political problems in the occupied territories but has many geographical deficiencies. The current boundaries of the city, delimited in 1967, were expedient rather than logical. Included in the city were Arab residential zones that never before belonged to it. The plotting of the boundaries was not executed carefully or with any geographical consistency. Israel wanted to include all the hills and ridges from which Jewish Jerusalen was vulnerable to artillery shelling by the Jordanians during the 1948-War. The reunified city extends to the fringe of the Judean desert on the east, to the airfield of Qalandiya in the north, and to the municipal limits of Bethlehem on the south. Israeli Jerusalem comprises an area 108 square kilometers, 2.8 times larger before the Six Day War (Fig. 6).

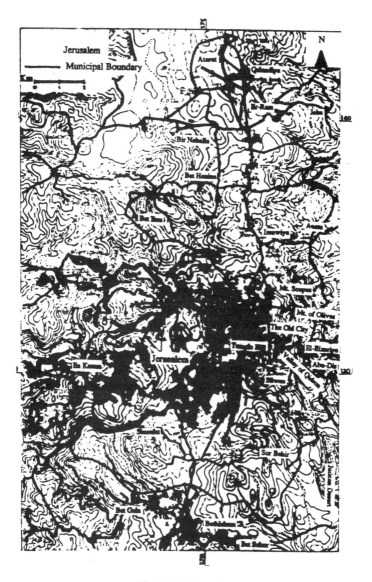

Fig. 6: Greater Jerusalem

The reunification of Jerusalem was marked by confiscation of Arab-held land and rapid construction of seven Jewish neighbourhoods. These residential locations partially encircle the pre-1967 city. Some governmental offices were shifted to East Jerusalem. The old campus of the Hebrew University on Mount Scopus was renewed and extended. A new industrial zone was opened in the north. The old Jewish quarter, destroyed by the Jordanians during the 1948–War, was reconstructed and repopulated with Jews. East Jerusalem was also a focus of rapid Jewish influx to re-establish claims to the former Jewish Quarter of the city and to assure access to the Wailing Wall, the most sacred place in Judaism. Even a few main roads were paved in Greater Jerusalem. On the other hand, no new Arab neighbourhoods were established, and no new institutions were created to serve the expanding Arab population.

In reunificating Jerusalem, the Israeli government intended to prepare the city to be the capital into which many Jews would immigrate to provide a counterweight to the rapidly expanding Arab population in the eastern part of the city. In 1967 there were approximately 196,500 Jews and 71,300 Arabs in Jerusalem, a proportion of 73.3:26.7. By 1994 the rate was 71.4 :28.6 with Jews numbering 400,000 and Arabs 160,000. As said, the annexation of East Jerusalem was twofold: to populate the newly annexed areas with Jewish inhabitants and to increase the overall Jewish population of the city. These policies were only partialy effective. The Israeli efforts to populate Jerusalem with Jews have not kept pace with the Arab natural increase, and demographic forecasts predict that by year 2000 the Arabs will constitute almost one–third of the city's population. On July 1980 Israel decreed Jerusalem to be its capital, a decision that ran counter to the policies of many foreign governments that objected it for political and religious reasons.

The building of new towns around Jerusalem as Efrata, Maaleh Edummim, Betar and Qiryat Arba marked a new stage in the metropolitan expansion of Jerusalem. The process of suburbanization in Jerusalem accelerated after 1977 with the right-wing Likud government who initiated the construction of several urban settlements around Jerusalem and channeled massive housing and development subsidies to them.

The very sensitive problem of Jerusalem is meanwhile not under discussion in the peace conferences. But after all, that is the most crucial problem in the area which has to be solved. Many countries and governments might be involved in it in the future.

Israeli-Palestinian Relations

Relations between Jews and Palestinians should be seen in conjunction with the associated increase of Palestinian labour in Israel. The 1967-War caused a process by which Palestinian surplus workers were integrated into Israel's space-economy. These are fixed Israeli Jewish workers and Palestinan workers as a 'nomad industrial reserve army'. Nowadays this army of workers reached approximately 120,000 people, most of whom commute daily from their homes in the occupied territories to Israeli employment centers. While they consist, though necessary, a 7 percent fraction of Israel's labour force, they consist about 50 percent of the Gaza Strip employees and 30% of the West Bank employees. Palestinians from the West Bank and Gaza Strip are integrated into Israel's economy in a way similar to Jewish commuters from the suburban towns in the occupied territories. But while the Jewish settlers are by and large middle class, the Palestinians were transformed into the urban working class, and their towns, villages and camps have become the working class suburbs, slums and poverty–stricken areas of Israeli's metropolitan regions.

A relationship has been created with a predominantly Jewish core, where production of value and surplus takes place, versus a Palestinian periphery with cheap labour force. This has altered the whole of the Israeli and Palestinian settlement system. Israeli employment fields and metropolitan areas extend deep into the occupied territories. Both Jewish and Palestinian settlements have become integrative parts of Israel's metropolitan regions. Both socio–national groups commute daily in the same roads network to employment centers, the Palestinains early in the morning, between 4.30–6.30, to building sites and garages, and the Israelis an hour or two later to offices and shops. 75% of the Jewish men and 65% of the women work outside the occupied territories. In the large city the Palestinians workers meet and interact with their Israeli neighbours but not at home. There in the street labour market and workplaces the Palestinians become conscious of their national and class identity.

Jewish Settlement and Settlers in Judea and Samaria

The future of Israeli settlement in Judea and Samaria is amongst the thorniest and most intractable problems confronting Israeli and Palestinian peace–makers, as they move to implement the September 1993 Declaration of Principles and the follow–up May 1994 agreement. To successive Israeli governments, these settlements have been a legitimate act of enhancing national security and restoring Jewish presence in their ancestral homeland, so as to prevent part of all these territories from returning to foreign hands. To Arabs and many international observers, the settlements have been a blatant violation of international law by an occupying power. The explosiveness of this perceptual gulf has been starkly demonstrated by numerous clashes between settlers and Palestinians over years, most notably by the Hebron massacre of February 1994.

By way of assessing the future of Israeli settlements in Judea and Samaria in the evolving peace process, this appraisal will trace the main stages of post–1967 Jewish settlement against the backdrop of the geographical, historical and political situation in the area, discuss the strenghts and weaknesses of this endeavour, and assess its resilience and viability (Efrat, 1994).

Background

Between 1949 and 1967 Judea and Samaria was bounded by the armistice lines between Israel and Jordan, with no physical or economic links connecting it with the State of Israel. In 1947 there were 264 Arab villages in Judea and Samaria, which had grown to 396 by the end of the Jordanian rule in 1967, a rise of 50 percent. The increase in rural population during the same period was even more pronounced: from 283,600 to 598,500, or 111 percent. This growth took place mainly in the Hebron and the Jerusalem districts, rather than in the northern parts of the region, probably as a result of the internal migration of refugees and the settlement of nomads. It should also be noted that before 1947 there was a normal distribution of the population among the villages, only few of which numbered less than 500 or more than 3,000 inhabitants (Fig. 7).

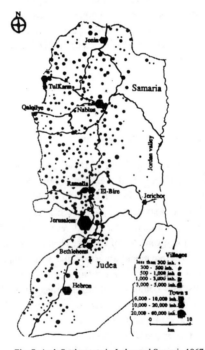

Fig. 7: Arab Settlements in Judea and Samaria 1967

Arab agricultural settlement in Judea and Samaria is a primary geographical phenomenon resulting from the physical nature of the region. The location of the villages, their distribution pattern, and the manner in which the physical conditions have been exploited to enable the inhabitants to sustain themselves and to preserve their way of life, may be taken into consideration by all new settlers in this region, even if equipped with modern technologies. Most villages are located on the mountain crest, a plateau favourable for agriculture, and on soft terraces with relatively deep soil; they take advantage of the local topography, avoid main highways and do not encroach on agricultural land. The traditional Arab village in the Judean and Samarian hills demonstrates the role played by the climate frontier as a barrier to the extension of villages, and explains the concentration and sedentarization of the population at the edge of the desert.

The distribution of towns coinsides generally with the watershed and follows the line of Hebron, Bethlehem, Ramallah, Nablus and Jenin. These towns constitute as administrative, commercial, marketing and service centers for surrounding villages, with Jerusalem having the additional function of being the regional capital (Elazar, 1982). All in all, traditional Palestinian settlement in Judea and Samaria has been wide–spread and deep–rooted, and has occupied most of the cultivable land.

Changes of the Settlement Map of Judea and Samaria after 1967

The sovereign territory of Israel as established by the 1949 Armistice Agreement ammounted to 20,700 square kilometers. The occupation of Judea and Samaria brought an additional 5,878 square kilometers under Israel's control, nearly a third of the country's territory. Prior to 1967, Israel's population stood at 2,750,000; following the Six Day War some 600,000 West Bankers, amounting 22 percent of Israel's population, came under occupation (Harris, 1980). Twenty eight years later this ratio has remained almost unchanged: 5.3 million Israelis, among them a million Israeli Arabs, compared with about more than a million Palestinians in Judea and Samaria.

The 'Allon Plan'

In 1967 the then Minister of Labour, Yigal Allon, presented the cabinet with a plan for the country's future borders, which proposed principles concerning peace arrangements with neighbouring states. The plan stipulated for a territorial compromise over Judea and Samaria that would meet Israel's security requirements while taking into account the aspirations of the Arab population. It proposed to leave some 40 percent of the area under Israel's sovereignty, with Israeli settlements along the Jordan Valley serving as a security belt. Though never adopted as an official doctrine, the plan exerted considerable impact on Israel's settlement map as long as Labour remained in power.

As early as 19 June 1967, less than a fortnight after the war, the Israeli cabinet decided to withdraw to the pre war lines in the Sinai Peninsula and on the Golan Heights (with exception of the Gaza Strip that was to remain in Israeli hands), in return for formal peace treaties and demilitarization of the evacuated areas. It was to change its mind, though, after the announcement of the famous three Nos – no negotiation, no recognition, and no peace with Israel by an Arab summit in Khartum on 1 September 19~7, and informed the United States of Israel's readiness to discuss essential matters with any Arab government.

To King Hussein of Jordan Israel offered a peace agreement but not on the basis of complete withdrawal. Shortly after the war it became evident that Israel was looking towards border modifications on the Jordan front, as illustrated by the Knesset's incorporation of East Jerusalem into Israel on 27 June 1967. The significance of the Allon Plan, which was conveyed to the King in person by Allon and Foreign Minister Abba Eban, in two secret meetings in London during 1968, this lay in its being the first comprehensive attempt to formulate a clear territorial stand regarding Israel's most problematic border, that with Jordan. The boundaries of the plan, derived from topographic and demographic considerations, were set between two longitudinal axes, one along the Jordan river, and the other along the eastern slopes of the Samarian hills; between them lay an arable and rather sparsely populated area. The 1967 census showed no more than 15,000 inhabitants, 5,000 of them in Jericho. The envisaged width of the proposed settlement belt along the Jordan valley ranged between 10 to 25 kilometers, and a security strip was to join Israel's sovereign territory through a broad stretch of several kilometers along the Jerusalem – Jericho axis (Allon, 1976).

The plan posited a large Jewish population in many settlements along the Jordan and the slopes of the Samarian hills, with agricultural settlements clustered around regional centers. The basis for this was the relative ecological advantage of the Jordan valley for early ripe winter crops and tropical fruits. The settlement of the Jordan valley was influenced by such factors as climate, the amount of water found locally, as well as the topographical features of the land. 37,500 acres of land were found to be arable. Other key considerations were proximity to the Jordan river to secure the eastern border, as well as to the longitudinal road; maximum population of uninhabited areas; and avoidance of occupation of land cultivated by Arabs (see prior Fig. 5).

In the run-up to the 1973 general elections the security retionale of the plan was underscored by Allon's fellow minister Yisrael Galilee, who drafted an ideological platform for the Labour Party, supporting the concentration of "security settlements" along the borders and rejecting Israel's return to the pre–1967 borders and the establishment of a Palestinian state in Judea and Samaria.

When conceived, the Allon Plan was a major innovation in Israel's strategic thinking. With the passage of time, however, it became outmoded. Rather than an asset, the concentration of settlements in a narrow strip of land came to be seen as a strategic liability that might restrict military manoeuvrabilty in the event of war; this scepticism regarding the utility of agricultural settlement as lines of defence in the occupied territories gained much ground after the October 1973 War, in which Israel was forced to hurriedly evacuate its settlements on the Golan Heights to prevent their seizure by the advancing Syrian army. Yet by 1994 Jewish presence along the Jordan Valley had expanded to some 6,000 settlers in 30 settlements, compared with about 30,000 Palestinians who own 13,500 acres of land.

The 'Gush Emunim' Settlements in Judea and Samaria

Settlement activity in Judea and Samaria has been carried out by Israel's two largest parties, Labour with its secular and socialist outlook, and the Likud with its religious and nationalistic stance. The former took a pragmatic approach to settlement, in the line with Allon's concept of defensible borders, avoiding settlements in densely populated areas. Likud, conversely, was committed to the territorial ideology of 'Greater Israel' and insisted on the right of Jews to settle everywhere in the territories, not least near major Arab population centers. A new kind of pioneer Zionism thus emerged, one that exhorted Israelis to exercise their rights in their historic homeland, and used nationalistic and religious justifications to this end. The "new settlers" had to be highly motivated, since the regions in which they settled were densely populated by Palestinians, a thing that made their endeavour a rather hazardous one.

The ultimate manifestation of these "new settlers" was provided by a new zealous established in 1974: 'Gush Emunim' (meaning "Bloc of Believers" or "Bloc of Faithful"). Emerging at a low point in Israel's national morale, shortly after the traumatic 1973–War, this radical excttra–parliamentary movement inscribed on its ideological flag the acceleration of settlement activity in the "Greater Land of Israel", Judea and Samaria in particular. The Gush's approach to the occupied territories was religious, indeed messianic. It was not only convinced of Jewish ancestral rights over Jerusalem, Hebron, Nablus, Bethlehem, shiloh and their like; it believed in the sanctity of the Land of Israel and maintained that through settling in its historic homeland, the Jewish people, and not only Israel, was nearing its salvation (Newman, 1982).

In practical terms, 'Gush Emunim' aspired to settle the mountain crest and the areas of dense Arab population. This meant the creation of territorial continuity between

33

Judea and Samaria and the State of Israel. The movement invoked the pioneering spirit that had animated the Jewish people in the past, and was evidently encouraged by the tradition that has developed in Israel whereby settlers had never abandoned their land by their free will. Their first actions were to revive the Etzyon Bloc, occupied by the Jordanian Legion during the 1948–49 War, and to reinstate Jews in Hebron, where they had lived for centuries, through the establishment of the suburb of Qiryat Arba. The growing influence of this young guard, mainly within the religious community, but also among Likud supporters, led to the demand that the government annex the occupied territories to the State of Israel.

The "Gush" embarked on its policy with a vengeance. Already in 1974 it established the settlement of Qeshet on the Golan Heights, and those of Ofra, Shiloh and in Kefar Kedumim in Samaria. As the Labour government was unable to agree on what measures should be taken against 'Gush Emunim', not least to the bitter rivalry between late Prime Minister Yitzhak Rabin and Defence Minister Shimon Peres, the movement could pursue its activities virtually undisturbed. In 1976 there were 220 'Gush Emunim' settlers in the territories, and it was clear that the government would not remove them. They even prepared an ambitious settlement plan of settling a million Jews in a hundred points in the course of one decade. The plan accorded priority to places on the Jerusalem Nablus axis, and two or three lateral axes traversing the mountain region. Its underlying principles were maximum spread of settlements; transfer of resources from the coastal plain to the hills; the establishment of a company to invest in industrial enterprise; rapid development of profitable projects; and state seizure of land whose ownership was unclear.

By 1977 'Gush Emunim' had already set up 12 settlements in the hills, comprising together some 500 acres of land. Each settlement consisted of few inhabitants, employed outside the area and commuting to Jerusalem or to the coastal plain; many settlers held on to their former dwellings as well. Likud's accession to power in May 1977 changed this modest beginning and gave the 'Gush' a tremendous boost. The late Likud leader Menachem Begin had never hidden his deep sympathy for this messianic extra–parliamentary group. He viewed 'Gush Emunim' as a selfless pioneering movement and, as head of the largest opposition party in the mid–1970s, supported their settlement activities. Now, with Likud in power, 'Gush Emunim' was rapidly transformed from a small disruptive force on the sideline of the Israeli political map into a mainstream movement.

Buoyed its new prowness, in July 1978 the 'Gush Emunim' prepared a second master plan for the settlement of 750,000 Israelis in Judea and Samaria, the first 100,000 by 1981. The plan envisaged two central towns, Qiryat Arba and Ariel, each with a population of 60,000 and four smaller towns of about 20,000 people each; this, in addition to 20 10,000–strong urban centers and 25 concentrations of community settlements. Through this extensive network of settlements the 'Gush' hoped to create an irreversible reality in the territories. Though it was obvious that such vast settlement activity would come at the expense of development in the Galilee and the Negev, and even on the Golan Hights, the Gush's grandios plan effectively became the official policy of the World Zionist Organization and Israel' Ministry of Agriculture, headed by the maverick Ariel Sharon.

During Likud's first two years 'Gush Emunim' succeeded in creating many facts on the ground, though the percentage of Jews of the total Judea and Samaria population remained practically low. Government policy sought to break up the territorial continuity of the Palestinian population by means of the Jerusalem area settlement in the center, those of the Jordan Valley in the east, and of 'Gush Emunim' in the heart of Samaria, in order to ensure that no autonomous entity above the level of local council would develop.

'Gush Emunim' created a new type of settlement, the community settlement, suited to the hills, with their scarcity of land and water; each such settlement comprised a few dozen families and was based on private initiative and partial cooperation, with no obligation to work in the settlement itself; this also suited many residents who had no agricultural background. By 1980 there were 18 'Gush Emunim' settlements in Judea and Samaria, and the next decade witnessed an extensive settlement effort in the hill country. By the time Israelis went to ballots in 1981, the 7,000 strong Jewish population in the occupied territories has trebbled. A decade later it exceeded the 100,000 mark (Fig.8)

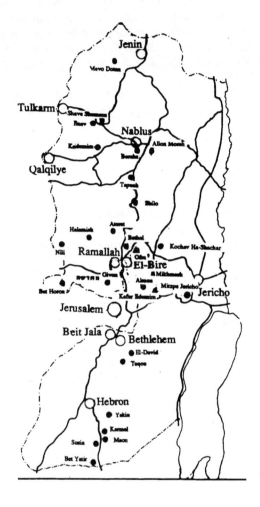

Fig. 8: Gush Emunim Settlemens in Judea and Samaria

One of the basic channels of the struggle over settlement is land, both as territory and as a source of livelihood. Since the land potential is absolute, each party wishes to take posession as much as possible: The Arabs cling to their land because it is ancestral, and because to them it means livelihood, happiness and honour. The Israelis, while sharing these basic aspirations, have hoped to detach the Arabs from their land and as practical means of settling in the area, for reasons of religious tradition, ideology, security and quality of life.

After the 1967–War an area of 1,445,000 acres of land came under Israel's jurisdiction. Only 30 percent of Judea and Samaria has been registered during British rule before 1947, mainly in the north of the Jerusalem – Jericho line. Where registration had been carried out, Israel could operate only on State land; this term covered virtually all categories of land, except that owned by local residents. Where no registration had taken place, and the ownership was not recorded, the government adopted a land policy based on the Ottoman law, which designated empty land, mountains, rocky areas, and rough terrain, unknown by anyone and unused by any city or village dweller, as dead consent, but the Sultan remained the absolute owner. The meaning of that law is that any land that is uncultivated or uncultivable, and is not recognized as private land, is State land. In view of the fact that 60 percent of the land in Judea and Samaria is not cultivable, and that a large proportion of it is unregistered, many areas could well be considered as State land. The Ottoman law allows exceptional rights on that land if a farmer cultivated it at least ten years. At the same time, the military government, with extensive powers regarding unregisterted land, operated on the basis of national and security needs, which very often resulted in legal confrontations between local and the Israeli authorities (Efrat, 1988).

Between 1967–1977, the ruling Labour Party implemented the old ideology of the Labour movement, which, since the days of pre–State has posited on an agricultural basis. This ideology was also applied to Judea and Samaria, which in turn necessitated the identification of fertile and arable land. By way of solution, the government either declared the land as belonging to absantees and leased it to the settlers, or seized it for security purposes. Likud's rise to power heralded a change in the concept of settlement across the 'Green Line' to one favouring settlement in all parts in Judea and Samaria. In 1979 Israel's Supreme Court issued a ruling that confiscation for military purposes could not be used for the establishment of a permanent civilian settlement. This in turn pushed the government in the direction of the Ottoman law. Rocky areas and unused land were pinpointed through aerial photography and declared as State land. As two thirds of the land were unregistered, and 60 percent were defined as uncultivable, a great deal of land was available for urban settlements on a relatively small area, with no need for an agricultural hinterland. Most of the Likud settlements were thus located on State land without impinging on privately–owned Arab land, and without expropriation for military needs.

To counter Jewish aspirations for control of the land in Judea and Samaria, Palestinians resorted to a series of means. This included the unsupervised extention of village areas by scattered buildings; construction in isolated spots unconnected with villages; and resumption of cultivation of abandoned fields. They seized State land and established faits accompli, in the hope of arresting the steady diminution of land with every new Jewish settlement. These activities were especially obvious around Jerusalem and along arterial roads, and enjoyed political encouragement and financial support from outside.

Plans for the Future Settlement in Judea and Samaria

As noted earlier, an ambitious plan for the settlement of Judea and Samaria, largely modelled on Gush Emunim's vision, was adopted by the Settlement Department of the Zionist Organization and Israel's Ministry of Agriculture. The aims were twofold, to settle 100,000 Jews in the territories between 1982–1987, and to increase their numbers to half–a million by the year 2010. The plan provided for the creation in the main urban settlements in the vicinity of the 'Green Line', that would be based on hard core of ideological settlers, as had been the case in the past; rather they would actually serve as residential suburbs of the Tel Aviv agglomeration and Jerusalem, offering their Israeli residents a high standard of housing at a relatively low cost.

An extended version of the plan proposed the preparation of land for 165 settlements over a 30–year period, so as to accomodate up to a million Jews in the territories. Five towns of 10,000–30,000 families each were to be established, as were 36 suburbs, each with 3,000 families; 65 communities of 400 families each; and another 60 collective and small holder settlements: The plan envisaged the construction of 5,000–6,000 units of dwelling per annum; the paving of 450 kilometers of roads; the expansion of the existing rural and urban settlements; the development of industrial zones at the rate of 100–125 acres per annum and continued acquisition of land. The areas identified for immediate implementation were Greater Jerusalem, the eastern slopes of the hills near Tulkarm, and south of Mount Hebron. The extended settlement plan did not concern itself with the empty areas east of the water divide, but aimed mainly at gaps between Palestinian villages on the eastern slopes. The model proposed was one settlement line to the east, loosely strung from north to south, and blocs of settlement to the west. The link between the blocs, and between Jewish settlements in the territories and pre–State Israel, would be maintained by a new infrastructure of local and national roads that would not be integrated into existing Arab roads and would allow for a settlement segregation.

To achieve the ambitious objectives, the plan divided Judea and Samaria into three 'demand zones' for residence and employment according to their distance from the metropolitan areas of Tel Aviv and Jerusalem. Areas within 30 minutes' commuting time from these centers, or ten to 15 kilometers east of the 'Green line', were defined as high–demand–zones; between 250,000–450,000 Israelis were envisaged to settle in these zones over a period of 30 years, or about 65 percent of the total Jewish population in Judea and Samaria. Areas within 50 minutes' commuting time to Tel Aviv or Jerusalem were defined as medium–demand–zones. The Jewish population in medium–demand–zones was expected to grow to 100,000–150,000 by the year 2010, while clusters of blocs of settlements in low–demand–zones were to accomodate between 40,000–70,000 Jews (Benvenisti and Khayat, 1988).

Conclusions and Consequences

For all these grandios visions and tireless toil, Israel's settlement ability in the occupied territories seems to be highly limited, both economically and demographically. The exorbitant investments in the territories have exhausted resources that could have otherwise been directed to development areas within the 'Green Line'. After 28 years of occupation, approximately 130,000 Jews lived in Judea and Samaria, as opposed to more than a million Palestinians: the gap between Jewish political and territorial aspirations and the actual reality remains very wide indeed, if not unbridgeable: not least, the fact that a mere three percent of Israel's Jewish population have settled in the territories affords a vivid illustration, if such were needed, of public reluctance to participate in this endeavour.

The Israeli–Palestinian Declaration of Principles of September 1993 has effectively brought the Jewish settlements in the occupied territories to their political and territorial end. Now they will have to play their last card following Israel's withdrawal from the territories and the establishment of a Palestinian autonomy, by ensuring some improvements for the future. In 1993 the Labour government froze further construction of houses in the settlements and prohibited the establishment of new ones; the settlers responded by adding infrastructure within the confines of their settlements and securing their commuting routes to 'Green Line' areas. Yet as the bilateral negotiations between Israel and the Palestinians unfold, the feeling that they may not be able to stay in their places of residence indefinitely seems to be dawning on most settlers. Many houses in the settlements remain empty, as no Israelis would consider moving to the territories in these uncertain times. Even more indicative of their growing anxiety within the Jewish community in the territories is the formation of settlers' organizations with the view to negotiating a fair compensation in the event of evacuation. The 1993 dramatic events, epitomized by the Washington accords and the ongoing bilateral peace talks between Israel and all its Arab neighbours, have apparently invalidated the widespread assumption among politicians and scholars alike of the irreversibility of the settlement fabric in Judea and Samaria. As the implementation of the first stage of the autonomy agreement in Gaza and Jericho approached, some Jewish settlers in the areas having lost faith in Israel's political and military authorities, began barricading their settlements for the eventuality of Israeli withdrawal; this probably being their last desparate act before disappearing from the stage.

It may be safely assumed that in the future fewer and fewer roads and even towns will be protected by the Israel Defense Forces, so that the way of life in many settlements may further be restricted. Only clusters of settlements adjacent to the Tel Aviv agglomeration or to Jerusalem will have a realistic chance to survive, while all the rest, mainly the remote and the small settlements, will disappear over time. After all, even a quick glance at the Judean and Samarian settlement map would reveal that only in 21 Jewish settlements, out of a total of 128, does the population exceed the one thousand mark; another 26 settlements comprise between 300–1,000 people, some 60 settlements – no more than 100–300 residents, while 12 include less than a hundred Jews; all the rest live in seven townlets. Put in a nutshell, 81 of the settlements, or 63.2 percent of all Jewish settlements in Judea and Samaria. have fewer than 300 residents not very comfort in thought given the trials and tribulations that lie ahead.

The Jewish population in Judea and Samaria has been widely spread, in line with past government policy of large distribution of settlements so as to capture as much land as possible. Only a few urban or semi–urban concentrations of settlements in the region are likely to play a role in the future redelineation of boundaries. Foremost among them are the townlets of Ariel, Immanuel, Elqana and Alfe Menashe, with their 30,000 inhabitants; the suburbs along the Bet Horon – Givat Zev — Har Adar axis, with 9,000 inhabitants; the townlet of Maaleh Edumim, east to Jerusalem, with its 16,000 people, and the Etzyon Bloc with its 8,000 settlers.

Undoubtly the settlers will have to fight for their survival in a region incredibly governed by the Palestinian autonomy. Some of them, those whose first homes in Israel are still available, will leave very soon. Others will leave when provided with alternative dwelling inside Israel itself, while a small group of extremists, the most ideological kernel among the settlers, will remain under Palestinian rule and continue to claim the rights of Jews to settle in all parts of Greater Israel. For how long these die–hard settlers will be able to last as a small island in a hostile ocean, and under what circumstances. remains to be seen.

Requiem of the Jewish Settlements in Judea and Samaria

Since the Oslo agreement which has been signed between Israel and the Palestinians in 1994, first symptoms of crumbling of the Jewish settlement layout in Judea and Samaria have been felt, expressed by organization of groups of settlers toward a possible evacuation of Judea and Samaria in exchange of financial compensation or fair alternative dwelling within Israel's 'Green Line' territory. Self organizations of that kind were already reported from Ariel, the biggest Jewish townlet in Samaria, from suburbs east and adjacent to the 'Green Line', and from some settlements in the Jordan Valley adjacent to the autonomous territory of Jericho. It may be estimated, that tensions appear among many other settlers, although not openly declared, but they may increase as the peace process will accelerate, and as the revolt of the Palestinians against the Israeli occupation in the territories will be stronger.

A possible crumbling of the Jewish settlement layout in Judea and Samaria could be expected a long time ago, and what was needed was a definite political situation to accelerate its process. The overwhelming refusal of extreme groups of Jewish settlers, and the resistance of Palestinians extreme groups, as the 'Hamas' and the 'Islamic Jihad', to the peace process, and the massacre in Hebron which occurred in 1994, created a situation from which a dynamic process of threat and unsafety in the occupied territory of Judea and Samaria has started.

Settlement in a geographical area for political interests by capturing a territory may succeed in certain conditions: when the number of settlers in the area is big enough to create a balance weight against the local inhabitants; when the settlers are able to form a considerable dense population which can keep successive connections among its parts; when the settlements in the area are established in a hierarchy according to size and function; when the settlement layout is executed by taking root on land, and most of the settlers are engaged in agriculture and local industry; and when the distribution of the settlements lean on main communications arteries which ensure free traffic between them. But what actually occurred was, that although many years passed since the first settlement establishment in Judea and Samaria, none of these basic conditions existed to justify Jewish settlement in this area.

The non–official number of settlers in Judea and Samaria is about 130,000, constituting not more than 12 percent of the Arab population, which does not create a meaningful balance weight against more than a million Arabs who live there. Even with the Jewish high birth rate in Judea and Samaria of 29 per thousand per annum, but as against 40 per thousand per annum of the Arab population, there is no chance to conquer the region demographically. Even the density rate of the Jewish population in Judea and Samaria is not very impressive. While the Arab density in this area is 179 inhabitants per square kilometer, that of the Jewish settlers is 22 only. The dispersion of the Jewish settlements in Judea and Samaria is unequal either. Although 128 Jewish settlements have been erected, a relative big number comparatively to the time since settlement in Judea and samaria in 1969 began, their distribution in the area remained very selective. Except in the Jordan Valley and in the Etzyon Bloc, where they demonstrate a full dominance on their territory, in all the other parts of the region it did not happen so. In northern Samaria their number is quite low, and so – in the western Judean Mountains and along the eastern flanks of Judea and Samaria. Their number is more conspicuous between Qalqilye and Nablus, and on the Bethel Mountains north of Jerusalem. Even if no congested Arab urban and rural settlement would exist in the region, it is doubtful whether such a layout of Jewish settlements could maintain reasonable economic and social interrelationship. Also the hierarchy of Jewish settlements in Judea and Samaria has not been developed systematically, and especially not in a right proportion between urban and rural villages. While a territorial distribution of settlements needs a hierarchial layout of towns and villages of different size, the reality is that in Judea and Samaria about 65% of the settlers reside in urban settlements which are almost equal in size, while the minority resides in small settlements with not more than a few hundred inhabitants in each. No primate town has been developed in the whole region as a capital. There are settlers who suppose that the townlet of Ariel in Samaria, whith its 14,000 inhabitants, is actually the capital of Jewish Samaria, but it is surrounded by a few other Jewish townlets, as Elqana with 3,300 inhabitants, Immanuel – with 4,800 inhabitants, Qarne Shomron – with 5,000 inhabitants, which compete to gain status as regional service centers in the region. Other townlets in Judea, as Qiryat Arba with its 6,500 inhabitants, Efrata with 4,000 inhabitants, and Maaleh Edummim, east of Jerusalem, with its 16,000 inhabitants, do not have direct relationship with the Samarian townlets and either not between themselves. Other smaller suburbs as Oranit and Alfe Menashe in western Samaria, or Pisgat Zev and Betar, which are located in Jerusalem's priphery, do not add very much to the Jewish settlement fabric in Judea and Samaria. Even the taking root on the land in most of the settlements seems to be very superficial. In most of the Jewish settlements along the western flanks of Judea and Samaria, and on the mountain crest, no agriculture has been developed, while industrial plants which were built in selected sites are not dominant as marketing centers for the region. Even in the Jordan Valley, which has good geographical conditions in climate, soil and water for early fruit agriculture, the production is not so high, and comparatively much lower than that in the Arava region, in the south–eastern Negev, a region in Israel's sovereign territory, which lies in more difficult geographical conditions and is remote from the central parts of the country. Even exclusive Jewish dominance on the main roads in Judea and Samaria was not achieved during the years. Although the paving of new crossroads in Samaria and Judea, both peoples are using them for their own traffic, which creates a situation sometimes very unsafety for both sides. In general, the sparse dispersal of Jewish settlement in Judea and Samaria unables linear and long–distance dominance by the existing road network, and more this network helped the settlers, more it has added to the commuting ability and the increase of motorization of the Palestinians (Fig. 9).

Fig. 9: Jewish Settlements in Judea and Samaria

Settlers according to Groups

The Jews who settled in Judea and Samaria for political reasons, and those who settled there because of convenience, the occasion to receive dwelling and land for a low price, beside utility and quality of life, are not of one piece. A study of their distribution in the region according to groups of settlers, that the militant and fanatic kernel among them, which organizes the demonstrations, makes noise and troubles to the military and political bodies, is proportional very small.

The division of settlers according to group and place of settlement could be elaborated according to some geographical criteria, as distance of their residence from Arab nationalistic centers in cities, and size of population in the different settlements. It was found, that the most fanatic extreme and nationalistic kernel of Jewish settlers lives inside some Arab cities or adjacent to their municipal boundaries. Such a kernel is, for instance, to be found inside Hebron, in the adjacent townlet of Qiryat Arba with its 6,500 inhabitants, around the synagoge site near Jericho, or at Joseph's grave in Nablus.

Another kernel, not less fanatic, whose origin comes from the 'Gush Emunim' movement of the middle 1970s, is to be found in two seperate concentrations. One is near the city of Nablus, in a rectangle whose corners are: Alon Moreh – in nort–east, Qarne Shomron – in north–west, Shilo – in south east and Elqana – in south–west. In this area, including townlets as Ariel and Immanuel, there exist about 20 settlements with 27,000 settlers. The second concentration of settlers is to be found in the Bethel Mountains, near the Arab cities of Ramallah and El-Bire, in a rectangular whose corners are: Ofra – in north–east, Halamish – in north–west, Almon – in south–east, and Bet Horon – in south–west. In this area there exist 15 settlements with a total Jewish population of about 9,000.

Except these two concentrations there exist in Judea and Samaria another three smaller ones, but less problematic from the point of view of political activities, because of their rural and suburban character. One of them is in the Rehan Bloc in north–west Samaria at the hinterland of the Eron Valley, with about a thousand settlers. A strip of settlements in a linear direction exists parallel and east of the 'Green Line', and includes about 15 settlements with 14,000 settlers. Another strip of settlements exists at the southern Hebron Mountains, including 15 settlements, between Telem in the north, Eshqolot in south–west, Karmel in south east and Maaleh Amos in the east, with about 2,5000 settlers.

Two other concentrations of settlers with less political and territorial involvement in their Arab surroundings are those of the Etzyon Bloc and the Jordan Valley, except a few settlements as Naama, Vered Jericho and others in the south, which were in 1994 disconnected from the settlement bloc of the Valley, because of the autonomy which has been approved to the city of Jericho. The historic Etzyon Bloc and its renewed settlements, including the townlets of Efrata and Betar, inhabit about 17,500 people, while in the 30 settlements of the Jordan Valley there are about 6,000 settlers, 1,200 of them in the townlet of Maaleh Efrayim.

Beside all these there exists a concentration of Jewish settlers near the municipal border of Jerusalem, with strong economic and social relationships to the city, although they reside officially in the territory of Judea and Samaria. The future of these suburban settlements should be connected politically with the destiny of Greater Jerusalem. Their population creates a suburban frame around the city, from Givat Zev and Har Adar in north–west, with their 10,000 inhabitants, up to Maaleh Edummim in the east, with about 6,000 people (Fig. 10).

Fig. 10: Proposed Clusters of Jewish Settlements in Judea and Samaria

45

The distinction between site and size of the groups of settlers indicates, that out of 130,000 settlers in Judea Samaria, about 30,000 are actually suburban dwellers of Jerusalem, about 22,700 live in the Etzyon Bloc and are included in a so–called national consensus not to be evacuated, and another 17,500 settlers are suburban dwellers along the 'Green Line' who do not arise special problems, because they will somehow be included in the sovereign territory of Israel when time comes to decide on. What remains is a group of 50,000 settlers who could be defined as zealots and as a potential problematic population. They encompass about 40 percent of all the Jewish settlers in Judea and Samaria, while 6,000 of them (4.6 percent) are concentrated in 3–4 points of territorial resistance.

The conclusions which could be drawn are: that the threathened number of settlers toward possible evacuation from Judea and Samaria is much less than declared. Most of the settlers' families have a high rate of children, so that the potential militant body is not greater than 10,000 people; their dispersal in the region and their small size which exists in most of the settlements reduces their reterrent force. Gradual evacuation of the settlers, when it will be decided upon, should be done at first in the problematic sites, then – in the two concentrations on the mountainous crest, so that the militant kernel will be neutralized, and the threat on the continuity of the peace process might be removed.

The Survival of Settlements

The agreement of principles which has been signed in Oslo in 1994, and the interim agreement between Israel and the Palestinians, concerning a gradual evacuation from Judea and Samaria while transfering autonomy to the Arabs in most of their administrative domains, leads the Jewish settlement in this region to a political and territorial end. If during a period of ten years, between 1967–1977, the settlers acted as a means for penetration into the occupied territories, with the aim to develop settlement and strenghten the so–called 'Greater Land of Israel', and if during a period of 15 years later, under the right–wing Likud government, they have achieved a maximal geographical and demographic distribution of their settlements in the Arab fabric, now they have to withstand their last political function which is, the existence and survival as a bargain card to play in the future negotiations with the Palestinians concerning final arrangements toward autonomy, the stages of withdrawal of Israel's military forces from the territories, and to achieve borderline revisions along the 'Green Line'.

While the government has freezed in 1994 the construction of new houses in the Jewish settlements of Judea and Samaria, and did not permit the building of new settlements, the settlers changed their activities, and as a reaction to the new regulations, started with an intensive completing of unfinished houses, reclaiming land and constructing installations within their settlement boundaries, according to plans which have been once approved, but not yet executed, and even collecting funds to strenghten their social services, paving access roads to adjacent settlements in the frame of regional self–organization to secure communications arteries connecting them with Israel's territory. All that has been done in case that the region might come under the regime of a Palestinian autonomy, and the possibility that Jewish settlements will be ruled by a foreign administration, to which they will have to measure on daily conditions of security, traffic and commuting. If till now the daily life of the settlers was managed with the inspection and assistance of the Israeli military forces, in future that situation might change, secured communications lines might be shortened and new political restrictions that will be created may encounter their future.

If may be assumed, that only bigger Jewish settlements in Judea and Samaria, which inhabit some thousand of settlers, will have some weight in the bargaining process concerning political and territorial border revisions, and that only those which have been developed to a meaningful size and were located adjacent to the 'Green Line', close to Jerusalem or Tel Aviv area, will have some chance to survive. The existing settlement map of Judea and Samaria does not ensure equal chances for all of them to survive, so that small settlements, and those which are located east and remote from Israel's 'Green Line', will not have any functional or territorial importance.

The Survival of Townlets

The Jewish population in Judea and Samaria counted in the year 1994 in its 120 settlements about 130,000 inhabitants, as against more than a million of Arabs. About 75,000 of the Jewish population in Judea and Samaria, or 62.5 percent of it, was concentrated in bigger townlets.

Regarding the areas of their distribution in Judea and Samaria it was found, that in the Jenin sub–district, for instance, there were about 1,350 Jewish settlers, mainly in rural settlements, and they constituted about eight percent of the total population. In the Nablus sub–district there were about 23,500 Jews – 11.5 percent of the total, most of them in the four townlets of Ariel, Maaleh Efrayim, Immanuel and Qedumim. In the Tulkarm sub–district there lived about 17,000 Jews, eight percent of the total, most of them in the suburbs of Oranit, Alfe Menashe, Elqana, Ginot Shomron and Shaare Tiqwa. In the Ramallah sub–dustrict there lived about 21,000 Jews, eight percent of the total, in the Bethlehem sub–district – about 24,000 (16 percent), most of them in the townlets of Maaleh Edummim, Efrata and Betar, while in Hebron sub–district – about 7,400 settlers (4 percent), most of them in the townlet of Qiryat Arba. The Jewish settlement was dispersed, however, in a large number of settlements, but with small populations in each, and that as a result of the former settlement policy of the right–wing Likud government, which encouraged the dispersal of many settlements in the area to create a 'faite–acompli' for a continuous occupation of the region in the future.

If only conspicuous urban townlets will have chance to survive in the future political situation under Palestinian autonomous administration, then good chances may be to Jewish concentrations of settlers in townlets as Ariel, Elqana, Oranit, Immanuel, Qarne Shomron, Ginot Shomron, Alfe Menashe and Shaare Tiqwa with their 30,000 inhabitants, which are located adjacent to the coastal plain and Tel Aviv area; some chance exists also to a line of settlements north–west of Jerusalem, between Bet Horon, Givat Zev and Har Adar with their 9,000 inhabitants; the townlet Maaleh Edummim, east of Jerusalem, with its 16,000 inhabitants; and also the Etzyon Bloc with its 8,000 inhabitants, after the execution of its planned connection with south Jerusalem by a new main road, by–passing the Arab cities of Bethlehem and Beit Jala. The settlements in the northern Jordan Valley may be integrated with the southern Bet Shean Valley, while the southern ones in the Jordan Valley will be disconnected from the rest by the autonomous area of Jericho. All the other settlements, which are located on the Samarian Mountain crest, on the their western flanks, on the Bethel Mountains, around Jenin or south–east of Hebron, will have no chance to be included in any agreement, that may enable them to survive under new political circumstances.

Undoubtly, the struggle for Jewish survival in the Palestinian future autonomous area will be hard and bitter. The settlcrs who still retain their former apartments and property within the boundaries of the 'Green Line', will certainly be the first to leave. After them there will be a group of settlers with no place to return to, and for them the government will have to find dwelling solutions within the sovereign territory of Israel, while a smaller number of settlers will certainly remain there and will refuse to be evacuated for any price, because of ideological and religous reasons, and will continue to keep its rights to live in the so–called fatherland even under Palestinian regime. In the settlement history of the Jews in the Land of Israel many episodes were recorded, as settlement trials in the Syrian Golan and the Jordanian Basan regions before World War 1, or that in Sinai in the 1970s after the Six Day War. It appears, that the present episode will be another one, but a more complexed and a more costly one.

Some latest expressions of Israel's ministers indicate, that after the agreement on the final status of the territories in Judea and Samaria many Jewish settlements will be uprooted, and all those which will survive will be able to exist and be included in two or three delimited settlement blocs. Until now, no delineated Jewish settlement bloc of this kind has been described, and no formal declaration has been given about the form of the future shrinked layout of Jewish settlements in Judea and Samaria.

According to the existing demographic and geographical wide dispersion of the settlements on the Samarian mountainous crest, and on its western flanks, the concentration of settlements in secured areas, with minimal friction with the Arab population, is very important. A process of achieving a shrinked settlement layout should be carried out according to the following principles: priority of existence should be given to blocs in which a relative high number of settlememts were established; creation of blocs around a town or townlet as an administrative and service center should be prefered; priority to blocs which are close to the 'Green Line', opposite to the coastal plain or Jerusalem; and periority should be given to linear areas with settlements connected by a main communications artery.

According to these principles it might be possible to delimit in Judea and Samaria a bloc of townlets aroud Ariel with about 40,000 inhabitants; the Etzyon Bloc will be to remain in its present shape with its 8,000 inhabitants; a narrow strip of settlements may survive north to Jerusalem with about 37,000 inhabitants; and some smaller ones at Rehan in north–western Samaria, or one in the southern Hebron Nountains.

If the minimal average distance between existing settlements in a bloc would be taken into consideration as a basic criterion for delimiting the main Jewish populated areas, then the blocs of Ariel and Etzyon may have chance to survive in the future political circumstances, together with the settled region in the Jordan Valley. All the others will have to disappear from the stage. Shrinked clusters of Jewish settlements will be the only outlet for Jewish further existence and survival in Judea and Samaria.

The settlement layout which has been created in Judea and Samaria for years with enormous governmental investment, is fundamentally spoiled, unlogical planned, and therefore has no chance for continuous existence. A settlement fabric, with based only on ideology, on an economic basis of services, and on the aim of territorial dominance cannot be religious commuting employment in Jerusalem or in Tel Aviv area. The collaps of such a settlement layout is only a question of time. This whole phenomenon in Judea and Samaria should be recorded in the history of settlement in the Land of Israel as another failed adventure which has been based on wishes and vision, and did not take at that time into account to a great extent the political complex relations that exist in this area.

Peace Patterns of Israel's Withdrawal from Judea and Samaria

Judea and Samaria, together with the Gaza Strip, might be considered an insurgent state lying adjacent to the official borderlines of the State of Israel. The people who live there want a country of their own in a territory currently dominated by a government in which they have no participation. To advance their case, the residents engage in various activities ranging from petitioning to terrorism. An insurgent state develops when a rebellious group secures and retains control of a territorial base of operations. The territory then becomes the basis for a state that performs most, if not all, with governmental functions and services (McCall, 1969). The Palestinians in Judea, Samaria and the Gaza Strip claim a significant geographical area as a national homeland.

Political developments which have recently occurred in the Middle Eastern arena, Israel's agreement to participate in bilateral and multilateral peace committees, the change of power in Israel's government since 1992 under the new leadership of Prime Minister Yitzhak Rabin, and the signed Oslo treaty from 1994, raise again the problem of 'territories in exchange of peace', which was under dispute between Israelis and Arabs and between Israelis themselves since 1967. While the subject has been discussed for a long time in a general or in a theoretical way, it seems that the Israel government will have to relate to it constructively in a more concrete manner, and introduce its clear and detailed positions. Israel will have to decide at a certain stage of the negotiations from which territories, except most of the Gaza Strip and Jericho, which was already given up, she will be ready to withdraw from, in order to achieve true peace with the Palestinians and her neighbouring countries, and which of the territories she will not be give up at any price.

The negotiations in the current periodically committees which are held, concentrate mainly on the Palestinian problem which is considered as the origin of the political conflict in this region. Wheras the Jerusalem issue is meanwhile not included in the agenda, and as the issue of the Golan Heights remains mainly a Syrian–Israeli problem, but not without its disregarded impact on the whole region, it comes out that the territorial problem in Judea and Samaria is the focus of the negotiations between the Israelis and the Palestinians, and according to that results peace in the region will rise or fall.

The purpose of this chapter is to demonstrate some geopolitical approaches to this problem, with the emphasis on the spatial perspectives and the geographical patterns from the Israel and the Palestinians points of view which may solve insurgency in the region (Efrat, 1992).

Background

The term Judea and Samaria or the West Bank identifies a political and administrative unit comprising two areas of western Palestine that came under Jordanian rule between the Armistice Agreement of 1949 and the 1967 Six Day War. After 1949 these areas were deprived of their contacts with the adjacent coastal plain and outlets to the Mediterranean Sea. Their sole remaining land contacts were thus with the Hashemite Kingdom of Jordan.

Judea and Samaria lies on the central massif of Palestine, with Judea region in an average elevation of 1,000 meters, and Hebron as its main urban center, while Samaria region has an average elevation of 500 meters, with Nablus as its main center. Judea and Samaria together encompass 5,878 square kilometers. Between them lies Jerusalem, a mountainous city under Israeli jurisdiction, and functions as the regional center for both Judea and Samaria.

Israel's conquest of Judea, Samaria and East Jerusalem in the Six Day War (1967) enabled to extend its frontiers, to improve its security and strategic position, and to realize what Jews perceive to be their historical rights to "All Land of Israel". After the Six Day War the territories became under Israeli military administration, and the previous orientation to Jordan has been partly replaced by linkages with Israel.

The geopolitical reality in the occupied territories, which exists since 1967 till today, emphasizes Israel's interests in the following domains: security, territory, water, demography and accessibility (Efrat, 1992a). Their relative importance for the security of the State and as a negotiable topic, is still a bone of contention among the public. Each of these domains has a meaningful geographical impact on the future of the State of Israel in its pre–1967 borderlines. If we assume that Israel's complete withdrawal to the borderlines of June 4th 1967 on one hand, and that permanent total occupation of Judea and Samaria on other hand, are both too extreme situations which might not lead to any positive solution when negotiations take place, some other alternative patterns should be introduced and related to possible scenarios of giving up some territories in exchange of peace with an emphasis on advantages and disadvantages for Israel's security and economy.

Territorial Patterns

One of the most important patterns toward peace settlement in this region indicates, that in order to secure the State of Israel from the east, a massive defence line is needed along the eastern flanks of the Samarian and Judean hills, opposite the Jordan River and the Dead Sea, although a full peace treaty has been signed in 1995 between Israel and the Hashemite Kingdom of Jordan. In 1969 the late deputy minister Yigal Allon expressed his opinion in that case and pointed out, that the western edge of the Jordan Valley should be based on a series of suitable topographic strongholds, making the greatest effort to avoid the inclusion of any large Arab population. The defence line must be based on a topographical system constituting a permanent obstacle for the deployment of motorized forces and a base of counter–offensive by the Israelis. It must provide the State with a reasonable strategic depth and ensure an early warning system (Yad Tabenkin, 1984). The area which fulfils such needs lies adjacent to the mountainous rural Arab settlement line in Samaria and Judea, and may form a buffer zone between the Arab population in the hill country and the Jewish one in the valley. For many years this area is being used as a military training zone comprising 250,000 acres, and is now too disrupted for settlement.

Another territorial pattern indicates the need of holding Jewish agricultural areas, that were settled in the past and form continuously an agricultural settlement region based on land cultivation, as an expression of Jewish rooting in the region, similar to the typical Zionist pioneering which took place in the Land of Israel before the establishment of the State (Fig. 11). Actually, there exists only two areas where such a kind of settlement occurred, namely the Jordan Valley and the Etzyon Bloc. As far as concerned to the Jordan Valley, the Isreali government accepted in 1969 the "Allon Plan" as a first comprehensive attempt to formulate a clear territorial stand regarding Jewish rural settlement in Samaria and Judea. The boudaries of that plan, derived from topographic and demographic considerations, were set between two longitudinal lines, the hills of Samaria in the west and the Jordan River in the east, where land was suitable for cultivation, and the area was sparsely populated. This approach was based on a regional settlement concept of development, with many agricultural settlements, and with Maaleh Edummim as a regional center. Agriculture in the Jordan Valley was based on a relative ecological advantage for early ripe winter crops and tropical items, climatical conditions, the available amount of water and the features of soil. About 30 Jewish agricultural settlements have been established since then, in which about 6,000 inhabitans reside. The valley can thus be deemed geopolitically, displaying features of attempting to settle a semi–arid area or a border region and establishing a settlement complex under harsh geographical limits.

Another region which fits that pattern is the Etzyon Bloc in the Hebron mountains, 20 kilometers south to Jerusalem, where 16 new settlements have been established after 1967 in which about 8,000 inhabitants reside. Since 1920 this region, purchased by a Jewish contributor, has been a target for Jewish rural settlement in the hill country of the Land of Israel. Three trials were made between 1927 – 1947 to settle this area through which four kibbutzim were established, based economically on hill farming. During the 1948–War the area was occupied by the Jordanians, and the four kibbutzim were abandoned. In a fourth trial made after 1967, the Jewish settlement in this region was renewed by youth whose parents had fallen in defence of the Bloc in 1948. New kibbutzim were established, and many other villages with the townlet of Efrata, as a regional service center (Katz, 1992).

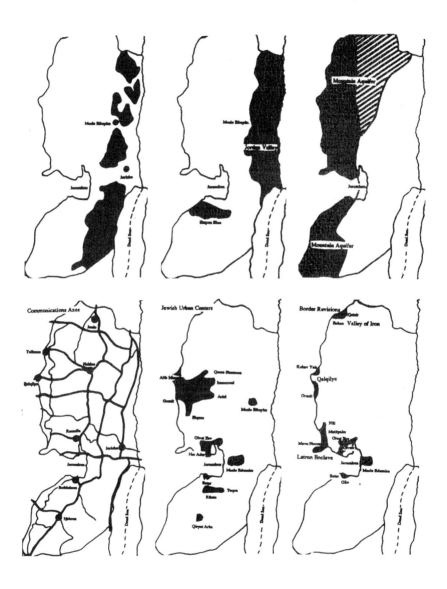

Fig. 11: Geographical Domains in Territories against Peace in Judea and Samaria

53

On the background of these historical events, it may be assumed, that according to the deep emotions of the Israelis to these two regions, one as a settlement plan in stage of being executed, representing the most important innovation on Israel's strategic and settlement conception, and the other, as a symbol of restoring to pristine splendour in the Hebron mountains, a consent exists among the Israelis to hold them for ever.

A third Israeli territorial pattern regarding Judea and Samaria indicates the importance of its underground water. The mountainous north–south backbone in Israel is a natural catchment area where underground water in aquifers is collected in basins. The hill aquifer of Samaria and Judea is the most important one for Israel because its water feeds the Yarqon and Tanninim springs at the western foothills, and a few others which are the main local water resources along Israel's coastal plain. The total water potential of the hill aquifers is 600 million cubic meters. The western and north eastern aquifers are overutilized, and yield an annual total of 475 million cubic meters per year (Benvenisti and Khayat, 1988). They supply about a quarter of Israel's annual water consumption. Overutilization has resulted a drop in the water table at a rate of 0.3–0.4 meters per year in the Judean aquifers. Overpumping affects water quality, causing increased salinity. Continuous overpumping could also make the underground water to sink below the 'red line' which decreases the usefulness of the aquifers. Israel is concerned about the future utilization of these water resources. The occupance and control of the resources by hostile forces are at the risk of Israel because they could be polluted by overpumping or by uncovering them to sewage. In that case the demand for the continuous holding of western Samaria and Judea by the Israelis could obviously be accepted.

Linear and Squatter Patterns

A pattern for holding Israel's sovereignty in this region indicates longitudinal and lateral axes of communications. Such axes should be delined generally in a gridiron form in order to connect predominantly Jewish population which is dispersed in small settlements and strongholds all over the area safeguarding territorial interests. Three such longitunidal axes, one along the Jordan Valley, between Bet Shean in the north and Jericho in the south, one on the hill country between Jenin, Nablus, Ramallah, Jerusalem, Bethlehem and Hebron, and a third one along the western flanks of the hills, together with Six lateral ones, which will be under Israel domain, may fulfil minimal security needs on the basis of linear accessibility, if no other territorial solutions are accepted. By a communications axis is meant, that a territorial strip of land, a few hundred meters wide, will be used for traffic, transportation and commuting through the region, while in these strips no further Arab building will be permitted (Efrat, 1982).

54

These axes may not superimpose existing roads that are transversing Arab territory, but should, as much as possible, by–pass towns, refugee camps, institutions and local civil instalations. The success of the existing lateral Samarian and Judean new roads, which were paved in recent years, support such a pattern which can provide security to Jewish settlements without occupying too much land.

The Six Day War influenced significantly the settlement geography of Israel. The greatest changes occurred in places from which the Arabs fled. After the war various groups of people who believed in hard line attitude to the Arab states, and in the retention of all the newly incorporated territories, came to the prominence in Israel's political life. The two major groups consisted of the right–wing Likud party and the religous nationalists of 'Gush Emunim' who were now the most prominent groups among the West Bank settlers. At the locational level, the new government gave a free hand to the activities to settle along the mountain ridge in Judea and Samaria. This area, constituting the center of the Israelite Kingdoms, has not been settled by the previous Labour government since it did not constitute part of their policy of establishing defencible boundaries, and also because this area contains the dense Arab population concentrations in the West Bank.

Quantitatively the process of settlement took the form of an exponential growth, with the year 1977 being the breaking point. It started as a return of Jewish inhabitants to the pre–1948 homes in settlements or neighbourhoods evacuated in the 1948–War, as the Jewish quarter in Old Jerusalem, the Etzyon Bloc and Hebron. Other more subtle forms followed later.

Jewish settlers in Judea and Samaria after 1967 confronted a population of 850,000 Arabs, who in course of time had occupied most of the sites for habitation. 128 settlements, containing about 130,000 Jews, have been established in the region by the Israeli government. These settlements constitute about three percent of the Jewish population in Israel.

A squatter pattern for this region indicates, that a number of Jewish urban centers, which were created after 1967, are a justification for holding urban territories. The biggest concentration of urban settlements exists along the eastern part of the coastal plain, between Qarne Shomron in the north, Elqana in the south, and Ariel in the east. This area was once of high demand for Jewish settlement, because it is defined as within 30–minutes' commuting distance from the outer ring of Tel Aviv, and within 20–minutes' commuting distance from Jerusalem or other towns in the coastal plain. It extends geographically 10–15 kilometers east to the former 'Green Line'. It has adequate roads connecting it with the larger cities and bringing it physically and psychologically closer to the population of the coastal plain. Its attractiveness caused an unexpected increase in its urban centers, as Ariel with 14,000 inhabitants, Qarne Shomron with

5,000, Immanuel – with 4,800, Elqana – with 3,300, Alfe Menashe – with 3,500, Oranit – with 4,100, and some other suburbs – with 1,000–2,000 inhabitants each (Central Bureau of Statistics, 1994). Other new urban concentrations exist around Jerusalem, as Har Adar, Givat Zev, Pesagot, Givon and Maaleh Edummim east to Jerusalem – with about 16,000 inhabitants. In the Judean mountains there exists the townlet of Betar with 5,500 inhabitants, and Qiryat Arba near Hebron with 6,500 inhabitants. The regional center of Maaleh Efrayim has about 1,800 inhabitants. In all these Jewish urban centers there reside about 60,000 inhabitants who comprise more then a half of all the Jewish settlers in Judea and Samaria.

A most significant explication process was the post–1977 wave of settlement which implied the most spatio–economic potentialities of the West Bank, namely, its close proximity to the metropolitan region of Tel Aviv and the city of Jerusalem. The migration flows originated in four major regions. The Tel Aviv metropolitan area, the city of Jerusalem, Israel's periphery in the Galilee, and in the Negev, and Jews from abroad. More migrants from Tel Aviv area moved to settlements in west Samaria region, while most migrants from Jerusalem moved to a group of settlements around Jerusalem. The Haifa area contributed its part to the settlement in north Samaria, while the Israeli periphery contributed mostly to west Samaria or the Jerusalem area. Jewish colonization of the West Bank was mostly part of the metropolitan expansion of Tel Aviv and Jerusalem. The development eastwards started mainly after 1977 as a consequence of the massive and rapid construction of new settlements on the western fringes of the Samaria mountains. These settlements were constructed as suburbs, devoid of a local economic base, as part of the declared government policy, to attract the occupied territories. This was implemented by large–scale investments in land purchasing, the construction of infrastructure and housing projects, and by declaring the whole of the occupied territories as development area. This implied high government subsidies for housing and generous loans to private construction companies and to investion of industries.

A more minimalistic territorial pattern indicates some needed border revisions along the 'Green Line'. Required revisions would affect the former Latrun enclave, the surroundings of Jerusalem, the surroundings of Qalqilye, and the Valley of Eron. The common factor to all these sections is, that during the years many Jewish settlements and suburbs have been established there which are now strongly linked to both sides of the former 'Green Line'.

Conclusions and Consequences

While exposing Israel's approaches to the possibility of territories in exchange of peace, it is quite obvious, that the Palestinians will refuse at the first stage to most of them, if not to all, presenting their standpoints concerning autonomy and sovereignty in Judea and Samaria.

Following the Israeli emphasized domains, as mentioned above, they may claim justly, that they own and cultivate half a million acres of land in north and south Samaria, in the hill country and its western flanks, where plantations of fruits and olives are dominant. They also need, not less as the Israelis, a free network of roads in this region without building limits, to strenghten their connections between Judea, Samaria and Jerusalem, and them – with the Gaza Strip in the west, and with Jericho in the east. Regarding water resources it should be indicated, that the Arabs own in this region 335 wells which supply 800 million cubic meters of water per year, and 300 springs which supply 40–60 million cubic meters of water. A hundred million cubic meters of water, out of 135 million, are used for agriculture. By Israel's intensification of water consumption they may loose their potential amount of water which is needed for agriculture. Concerning the Israeli squatter patterns of settlement they may also claim, that Arab urban concentrations exist in Judea and Samaria for a long time. In them there live about half a million inhabitants, many of them in suburbs. In this region there even exist about 400 Arab settlements which indicate a spatial dominance all over the region.

In a direct negotiation process no side will be able to receive all what he wishes, and therefore compromises will be needed on the basis of these territorial patterns. It could also be assumed, that no single pattern will be dominant throughout the negotiation process, and that some variations of them may be accepted. However, there is no doubt, that a comprehensive approach to these patterns on the basis of 'territories in exchange of peace', enables a rational selection of priorities for each side towards the achievement of an agreement, its stages of implementation, the timing of its execution, and the testing of each sides' seriousness and intentions to peace and to the normalization of the region. These patterns may also provide politicians and decision makers with guidelines to enable Israel's gradual withdrawal from Judea and Samaria, or at least for an interim agreement if needed. After 28 years of Israeli rule in the territories, and more then seven years of an active and violent Palestinian uprising, no workable political solution has yet been proposed. Only a scheme with clearly delimited political, geographical, demographic and military characteristics can promise fulfilment of the two peoples' aspirations and bring peace to the region. It seems, that the fundaments of peace achievement with the Palestinians and the neighbouring countries lies in both sides' attitude to the insurgent region of Judea and Samaria.

'Intifada' – the Geography of a Palestinian Political Uprise

December 9th markes every year the day when Palestinian uprising against the government of Israel in the territories of Judea and Samaria and the Gaza Strip began in 1987. This uprising ('intifada' in Arabic), which came as a great surprise to the Israelis, grew out of an array of Arab political motivations: the quest for Arab self–determination, their demands for an independent Palestinian State, and the evacuation of the Israeli military forces from their territories. The uprising began with an incident in the Gaza Strip and spread quickly to other locations in Gaza and Samaria, and eventually assumed the character of a violent revolt throughout the Palestinian Arab areas. The geography of this uprising can be traced by noting its regional characteristics, by identifying its various stages, analyzing its critical locations, and examining the demographic and other spatial aspects which gave it direction (Noble and Efrat, 1990).

The Nature of the Palestinian Uprising

The Palestinian uprising began very suddenly and quite unexpectedly. The initial incident was a car accident which occurred near Gaza between an Israeli vehicle and an Arab vehicle, in which three Arabs lost their lives. The Arab popuplation claimed, that it was an accident caused by the Israeli. This meaningless unimportant incident ignited a reaction which led to a political uprising, not only in Gaza but in Judea and Samaria as well.

The deeper and more widespread reasons of the uprising were three: the basic Arab hostility to the Jews, whom they consider to be an alien people, and to the continuing existence of the State of Israel; continuing demands for the right of all Arabs who live in refugee camps, to return to their pre–1948 lands; and an internal spontaneous expression of feelings of frustration and an expression of the state of mind of a population who see as discriminated against, and who perceive little or no possibility of positive change in future.

To these main causes a few more specific reasons could be added: physical overcrowding and lack of facilities and economic opportunities in the refugee camps; a gradual decline in the economic opportunities of the entire Arab population; a continuing and widening disparity in the standard of living between Jews and Arabs; the low standard of physical infrastructure, including electricity, telephones, roads and engineering installations within the occupied territories; fear that the continuous development of Jewish settlements in the territories and the ongoing process of Arab land confiscations is designed to promote eventual Israeli political control; frustration of educated persons, who remain unemployed or employed in low–paying and low status

58

manual work; bureaucratic barriers and annoying restrictions in daily life under hostile military administration; and a feeling of helplessness resulting from the total dependence on Israel, which dominates the local economy in the territories.

Whiles none of these specific reasons by themselves might have provoked a reaction, collectively they provided a rationale for inciting the population in the territories to strike, to demonstrate, and to initiate disruptions and disturbances in the routine of life. Arab leadership committees, through a series of proclamations, encouraged the population to continue the uprising day–after–day. The Palestinians were exhorted by their local leaders to make personal sacrifices by opposing the Israeli administration, although that action ultimately harmed the inhabitants themselves by poromoting reaction by the Israeli military. The uprising also was expanded by Arab attacks on soldiers, by throwing stones, and even bombs, at passing Israeli vehicles, by destroying crops in Jewish fields, and by harassing, and even murdering Israelis when an opportunity was presented.

On the other side, the Israelis took steps to require the Arab population to obey military orders and regulations. Administrative and economic pressure were jointly applied, and military actions were implemented, such as the immediate dispersion of demonstrators, massive arrests and prolonged curfews. In extreme cases, the homes of suspected uprising participants were blown up or bulldozed. By these steps the Israelis tried to regain control whithin the territories, with the hope of weakening the Arab population by intimidation and to force them to turn their back on the leaders of the uprising. Actually, as the uprising went on, more Arab inhabitants joined it, and many more passively supported it as hostility grew to the application of Israeli force.

The continuous turmoil in Judea and Samaria and the Gaza Strip has changed significantly the whole geopolitical situation in the territories. Certain geographical and spatial features enabled the uprising to develop, spread, and continue for a long time, and even succeeded. Spatial dispersion of the Arab population, the scatterd and defensively favoured sites of towns, the dispersed layout or form of the settlements, the network of roads, the location of Israeli settlements in the territories and the artificial reunification of Jerusalem, were among the main geographical phenomena which reinforced or affected the uprising. The influence of these phenomena may be observed in the context of three different themes: the demography of the Arabs in the territories; the location of the refugee camps; and the characteristics of the reunificated city of Jerusalem.

The Demography of the Arabs in the Territories

Most of the Arabs of the West Bank reside on the wide crest of the Judean and Samarian Mountains, and are well dispersed in hundreds of villages located on hilltops and ridges from where they easily dominate their surroundings. The Arab population has spread continuously westwards in the direction of the boundaries with Israel. The largest towns are situated on the mountains axis between Hebron in the south and Nablus in the north, while other towns, such as Qalqilye and Tulkarm in the west, and Jenin in the north, are often adjacent to the 'Green Line'. Jerusalem, surrounded by several smaller towns and villages, contains the largest concentrations of Arabs. Between Ramallah and el–Bire to the north, el–Eizeriye to the east and Bethlehem, Bet Jala and Beit Sahur to the south, reside about 150,000 Arabs, in addition to 160,000 in East Jerusalem itself. In the Gaza Strip the geographical dispersion of the population is even more unequivocal. The inhabitants there occupy all the fertile land and more than 80 per cent of the area.

According to military census held at the end of the Six Day War in 1967, there were about 595,000 inhabitants in Judea and Samaria. This population increased to more than a million in 1994, a growth of 76 percent. While in 1967 about 225,000 inhabitants of the West Bank lived in the 12 largest urban places, in 1994 about 560,000 resided there, a growth of 100 percent; and while the proportion of urbanization in 1967 was 27 percent only, at the end of the 1980s it had grown to 150 percent. These figures indicate a rapid growth of the Arab population in Judea and Samaria, and that urbanization trends have intensified. Even the rural population, which is dispersed in more than 400 villages of various sizes, grew rapidly since then, and many villages gained the status of municipalities (towns).

The main reason for the permanent growth of the population is the very high natural increase among the Arabs, about 37 per 1,000 per annum, against 19 per 1,000 among Jews. The Arab population is much younger than the Jewish. More than half of the Arab population in the territories is under five years old! This figure promised even higher population totals in the future. To that should be added, the facts that the Arab population still live together in large extended families, the attachment to their land does not encourage them to emigrate, and the possibility of steady, albeit manual work in Israel provides a modest economic security.

In the Gaza Strip, the demographic situation is evem more striking. In an area of 363 square kilometers, which is 1.75 per cent of Israel's territory, or 6.2 percent of Judea and Samaria, were some 800,000 inhabitants (1991) in a density of 2,200 persons per square kilometer, against 171 in Judea and Samaria, or 251 in Israel. The natural increase in the Gaza Strip is 4.8 per 1,000 per annum, higher than in any other Arab country, and among the highest in the world. Most of the inhabitants in the Strip reside in the four towns of Gaza, Khan Yunis, Deir el–Balah and Rafah, in eight large refugee camps, and in many smaller villages. About half of the Strip's population are refugees. Against the 800,000 Arabs who reside in the Strip, there are about 5,300 Jews dispersed in 16 agricultural settlements, most of them in the Qatif Bloc at the south, which occupy about 15 percent of the Strip's territory.

Israel tries to mitigate the fact of Arab demography by encouraging Jews to settle in Judea and Samaria and in the Qatif Bloc. The government subsidizes settlers by providing modern apartments at low prices; the settlers get special deductions in income tax, they receive loans on convenient terms, and all their infrastructure of their settlements is built by the Ministry of Housing. The Arabs, on the other hand, must rely only on their high birthrates with no governmental, economic assistance, but their 'demographic' strategy in the long run pears likely to be successful.

The Dispersion of the Refugee Camps

According to uncertified UNRWA data there are in Judea and Samaria about 943,300 Palestinians, and about 536,600 in the Gaza Strip, for a total in all the territories of about 1,479,900. The assumed number of refugees in the West Bank is about 107,000, dispersed in 20 camps between Jenin in the north and Hebron in the south. In the Gaza Strip the number of refugees is even higher, about 260,000 in eight camps, dispersed between Jibalya in the north and Rafah in the south (Fig. 12).

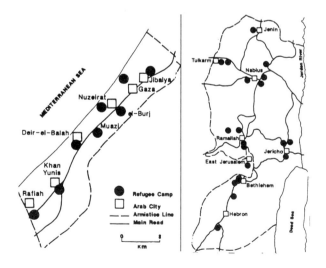

Fig. 12: Refugee Camps in Judea, Samaria and the Gaza Strip

61

These figures indicate that the total number of refugees in the administered areas is about 367,000, and they comprise a quarter of the total Arab population. Although the biggest concentration of refugees is found around Nablus, the capital of Samaria, almost all the camps, especially in the Gaza Strip, are large, containing 40,000–50,000 inhabitants each. About half the Gaza Strip's total population are refugees, who still live in camps. Almost all camps in the Strip are bigger than their adjacent towns or villages; all the camps located near towns spill over their boundaries creating large squatter settlements around them.

Since the 1948–War none of the refugee camps has been removed. To the contrary, they have become an integrated part of the landscape and permanent settlement for a population homogenous in origin, culture, and condition. In large part, the refugees in each camp originated in a single, abandoned village, a region or even extended family, and have maintained structure and relationships from their earlier settlement and condition. The camps were built on what once was vacant land near Arab towns and along main traffic arteries, because of the need to supply the refugee population with work, physical facilities, and urban services support. Ease of access also makes the camps easier to control. A small number of refugee families, mainly the richer and more educated ones, have left the camps from time to time and been absorbed into nearby cities, or they emigrated to Jordan and other foreign countries. Those who remained behind are poorer families, supported largely by the UN Refugee Welfare Agency and the new administration authorities founded by the Palestinians in the Gaza Strip since 1993.

While the camps were not expanded, the natural increase of the population has caused greatly increased population densities and the spilling over of the camps to surrounding land. The quality of life in the camps has worsened steadily over time. As population has increased, building density also has gone up, but without any conspicuous improvement of the physical infrastructure of the camps. Indeed, the opposite has occurred. Thousands of houses made of clay have been erected, but water suply, sanitary facilities and solid waste disposal have not been provided in a similar ratio. Most critically, few sources of employment for the expanding population have been created in or near the camps.

When a quarter of the population of the territories lives in conditions such as these, with a partial political identity, and which has developed in the Gaza Strip and Jericho after the Oslo Agreement, with no valuable political solution in prospect, their frustration steadily rises. It is no surprise that such frustration is used by national, local and external bodies as a point of agitation against Israel, which the refugees blame for their cruel fate. When that time arrives when the refugees in their camps reach a dead end, with nothing further to loose, they gladly take upon their shoulders the main political struggle against Israel as demonstrated lately in terrorism and the extremists' attacks of the 'Hamas' and 'Jihad' groups.

Spatial Aspects of the Uprising

A spatial analysis of the events which took place in Judea and Samaria and the Gaza Strip since the beginning of the uprising indicated that the incidents had geographical and demographic aspects, and therefore could be expected to happen in certain critical places and areas.

If we examine the large number of places where violent events have happened during the uprising, we find the following common characteristics: almost no events occurred on the eastern flanks of the Judean and Samarian mountains, nor in much of the Judean desert; almost no violent activities appeared in small villages in western Samaria and Judea, where many agricultural settlements exist, quite remote from the main towns; violent activities appeared early in towns and villages which are located on the mountainous crest in Judea and Samaria, and especially along both sides Jenin axis; the most of the Hebron –Ramallah – Nablus serious disturbances arose in the business districts of the bigger towns, and in adjacent larger villages; the greatest violence appeared in towns which were surrounded by refugee camps, and in the camps themselves; in the Gaza Strip the big refugee camps were the earliest and most active focii of violence, and among the towns, Gaza and its refugee camp esh-Shati, were the leading ones; the greatest focus of violence during the uprising was in Nablus, the capital of Samaria, and its surrounding camps; in Judea there were only a few early focii of disturbances, mainly along an axis of large villages on the eastern and southern rim of the crest; perpiheral towns in Judea and Samaria, such as Qalqilye, Tulkarm and Jericho, which lie adjacent to Israel's boundaries, became important local centers of violence; the surroundings of Jerusalem became a "Ring of Fire" which extended from Ramallah in the north, Abu–Tor in the east to Bethlehem in the south; remote but large villages on the crest did not take generally part in the uprising, but some small villages in the periphery were very active; all centers of violence were adjacent to the main roads in their region and in places where the friction with Jewish population was intensive.

In addition to these common characteristics of the places where the uprising evolved, at last four stages or phases in the development of the uprising were identifiable (Figs. 13 and 14). The first stage, which comprised the first two months of the conflict, produced widely scattered incidents of violence. During this early phase, three centers – Gaza Hebron, and Nablus – evolved as the principal focal points. swift action by the Israeli government to alleviate some of the basic conditions which acted as cause of the violence might have confined the uprising to these centers and brought it to a rapid conclusion.

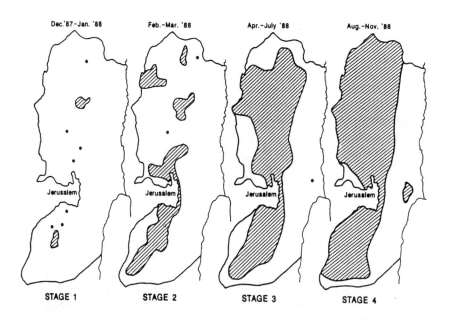

Fig. 13: Stages of Intifada in Judea and Samaria

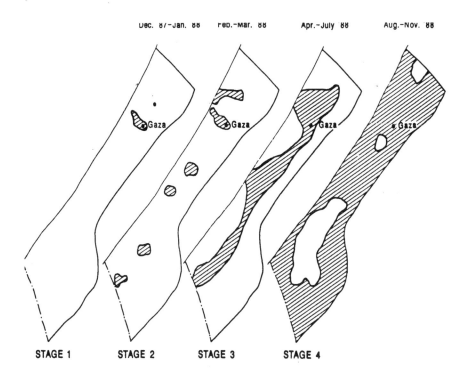

Fig. 14: Stages of Intifada in the Gaza Strip

65

By February and March 1988, stage II was developing, involving an initial proliferation of violence to areas surrounding the three original centers and to a number of additional places. In Gaza these points were the Palestinian Arab refugee camps. In Samaria and Judea a similar aerial pattern occurred, but with somewhat greater orientation to the main north – south transportation route.

In stage III, the various isolated centers of conflict had coalesced, therby permitting mutual support between formerly seperated centers. Control of lines of cummunication became a major objective of the contesting parties, although Israeli force was usually sufficient to ensure domination, at least in daylight hours.

Stage IV was attained between August and November 1988. In this latest phase virtually the entire area of both Gaza and the West Bank has become enveloped in the uprising. The openly significant areas not affected were the Jordan Valley and the Bedouin–occupied areas of the eastern Judean desert. The uprising had become so pervasive, that only a major policy shift by the Israeli government seems likely to be able to solve the difficulties.

The Arab urban population in Judea and Samaria has been traditionally the more educated and the more nationalistic and political–minded, which helps to explain why towns in that region became the leading focii on the uprising. On the other hand, the refugee camps contained the most frustrated and poorest population, which also explains why they appeared as centers of violence.

The implentation of Israeli settlements into areas of Arab towns and villages, and the pervasive Jewish populating of the territories, introduced a kind of demographic tension. The topographical priority of the Arab settlements on the mountainous crests, and on the better–watered flanks, and the dominance of the Arabs on the main roads and over most of the territory, provided a strategic base to support the Palestinian uprising. The growing Arab encirclement of Greater Jerusalem, and the artificial reunification of that city, perhaps unnaturally combining two peoples who have little in common, also produced a source of discontent fostering unrest (Romann, 1981).

The Reunified City of Jerusalem

Jerusalem is an example of the problem which have led to the Palestinian uprising. The boundaries of Jerusalem, which were delineated in 1967, were expedient rather than logical (Efrat and Noble, 1988). They included too much mountainous area and too many Arab neighbourhoods and suburbs which had never before belonged to the city. By delineating these particular boundaries, Israel's purpose was to include all the hills and ridges from which Jewish Jerusalem had suffered artillery shelling by the Jordanians. The boundaries of reunified Jerusalem extend up to the western fringe of the

Judean Desert in the east, to the airfield of Qalandiya in the north, and to Bethlehem in the south. Jerusalem comprises an area of 108 square kilometers, 2.8 times greater than that of the city before the Six Day War. Only the western boundary abuts territory which was part of Israel between 1949 and 1967.

Among other techniques, the reunification of Jerusalem was accomplished by confiscation of Arab land, and by a rapid construction of seven new Jewish neighbourhoods. These residential settlements were built at strategic locations partially encircling the pre–1967 city. On the other hand, no new Arab neighbourhoods have been established in East Jerusalem since 1967, and no institutions for the benefit of the growing Arab populatin have been created.

Israel's intention by the reunification of Jerusalem was to prepare the urban area as a capital to which many Jews would immigrate and increase, thus providing a counterweight to the rapidly expanding Arab population in East Jerusalem and its surrounding area. Since 1967 the Arab population has gradually increased, but the efforts made by the Israelis to populate Jerusalem with Jews have not kept pace with the Arab natural increase.

Conclusions

This chapter has undertaken a brief analysis of some of the the geographical characteristics of the uprising in Judea and Samaria and the Gaza Strip. It was attempted to present them illuminating a delicate and critical political situation. Geography has played a meaningful role in the dynamics of the uprising in the components of sense of place, direction of action and, intensity and duration of resistence.

Altough the uprising started at a geographically random point of contact, it accelerated and advanced rapidly in a rational and logical fashion and even brought to terror. The rate of advance and intensiveness of the uprising depends very much on the location and dispersion of points of friction. When the leaders of the uprising aspire to gain territory it concentrates mainly on topographical and strategic places, along main communications arteries and administratative and political boundaries. The focii of the uprising are greater and stronger in cities and in other urban agglomerations such as the refugee camps, this in remoter villages or the countryside itself. Concentrations of deprived and hopeless people are ideal centers for agitation. Once the uprising developed within such areas and along such axes, it spread simultanously both by expansion and in relocation to discontinuous areas.

After many years of Israeli rule in the territories, and more than eight years of an active and violent Palestinian uprising, no workable political solution has yet been found in this region. As a political rigidity on one side, and the activism of the uprising on the other, no way remains other than facing the fact, that the two peoples have to exist within the "Land of Israel", side by side, with defined boundaries between them. Only such an existence with clearly defined political, geographical and demographic characteristics can promise the fulfillment of the two people's aspirations and bring peace to a significant realm of the world.

The Revival of the 'Green Line'

The signing of an agreement between Israel and the Palestinians in 1994 regarding autonomy in the Gaza Strip and Jericho, naturally arises the main problem of Judea and Samaria, which is now under negotiation toward the establishment of a Palestinian State. This issue renewed the tension between the Israelis and the Palestinians in the region and will sharpen the security and economic conflict between Jews and Arabs in future. In all the possible alternatives of spatial agreements in the region the Israelis relate a great importance to the 'Green Line' as a security and ethnic borderline between them and the Palestinians, because of the danger of terror attacks on Israel which may initiate from the future autonomous territories.

The 'Green Line' as a border between Israel and Jordan, was established after Israel's War of Independence in 1949, and seperated Judea and Samaria and the Gaza Strip from the rest of Israel's territory. This line was thickened in the past by the establishment of the so–called 'Nahal' settlements along it, populated by army units who combined security and military training with agricultural work. The line, in a lenght of nearly a thousand kilometers, has been supported by new development regions that were established along it, such as Lakhish, Besor, Taanach and the Arava region, mainly for the purpose of reinforcing border strips of land. The 'Green Line' was very dominant as a border between the two countries during the years 1948 – 1967, till the outbreak of the Six Day War in 1967, which changed the region politically and territorially. Israel unilaterally recognized then the Jordan River as its eastern border, conversed unilaterally the armistice line in the Golan Heights into a security border, and created a de–facto border between Israel and Lebanon in the form of a narrow security zone, north of the 1923–international borderline.

In the last years, as terrorist attacks initiated by the extreme Arab political groups of 'Hamas' and the 'Islamic Jihad' became more frequent, the 'Green Line', which after 1967 had to be vanished according to the Israeli policy of `Greater Land of Israel', that insisted upon, that no inner borders will exist within the whole territory, had to renew its security functions as a zone line to secure Israel's population. It was realized, that the 'Green Line' was actually a broken border with many geographical and demographic shortcomings, which stem from its history of the years 1948 – 1949, when it was first delineated, and the geographical changes which occurred along it since the Six Day War in 1967. Its weakness as a defence line for Israel may be demonstrated in four main domains: its big lenght; its twisted delineation on a difficult mountainous topography; the large Arab population which resides on both sides of it, with the Palestinians on its east side and the Israeli Arabs on the west; and the relative sparse Jewish population which settled adjacent to it through the years.

The 'Green Line', which has been finally delineated in 1949 as an armistice line between Israel, Egypt, Jordan, Syria and Lebanon, was actually a cease–fire line agreed upon in Rhodes, and approved by military representatives of all the partners who participated in the 1948–War, with the mediation of UN observers. It expressed, more or less, the military situation of the positions that existed at a certain moment of cease–fire, but it had not many security elements in it which could promise full defence to Israel from Arab infiltrations and terror attacks. It was delineated at that time with unsufficient data on the geographical characteristics of the regions through which it had to run. In the south of Hebron Mountains, for instance, it was marked on the high mountainous ridges of Dahariye and Eshtemoa, 500 700 meters above sea–level; in the Jerusalem Mountains it dissected in a diagonal way mountainous ridges 700–800 meters high; in northern Israel it bisected the Amir Ridge 400–500 meters high, and the Gilboa Mountain – in a longitudinal section. It was obvious that in such twisted topographical conditions the line will not be able to defend Israel's sovereign territory. Furthermore, the 'Green Line' encircled in its delineation in Judea and Samaria an area of 5,878 square kilometers, which means, that every kilometer of borderline may protect an average hinterland of about 23 square kilometers, which demonstrated actually its big lenght relative to the territory which it comprised.

In addition to that, the 'Green Line' was dissected by more than 50 wadis of different width, five of them running in the valleys of Bet Shean and Harod, four – in the Valley of Eron, about 20 – in the Judean Mountains, and all the rest in the southern Hebron Mountains. Most of them are dry streams of the rivers Bezek, Hadera, Alexander, Yarqon, Soreq and Beer Sheba. They are used by the Palestinians as relative easy infiltration axes, and while they are dry during most of the year, their effectiveness for this purpose is obvious.

Regarding the Arab population which resides along both sides of the 'Green Line' it should be indicated, that at the time when the line was marked, there lived along it in Judea and Samaria about 100,000 people, while today the Arab population which lives in a distance of 2–3 kilometers east of the line, counts about 190,000. On the west side of the line, in the same width, but in Israel's territory, there live about 100,000 Arabs which have direct interrelationships with the Arab people in Judea and Samaria, and by that actually blur its ethnic character. This can be found especially in north and north–

west Samaria, opposite to the Hadera–Afula communications artery of Eron Valley, and opposite to the central coastal plain, between the Arab villages of Baqa el–Garbiye and Qafr Qasem. A more substantial ethnic seperation between Jews and Arabs along the two sides of that line exists in the Jerusalem Corridor, in western Judean Mountains and in the southern Hebron Mountains.

The Jewish population which resides adjacent to the 'Green Line' in Israel's territory, in the same distances of 2–3 kilometers west of it, counts only about 35,000 people, while that on the eastern side of the line in Judea and Samaria about 28,000 settlers. It means, that the Jewish population along both sides of the 'Green Line' finds itself in a big gap comparatively to the Arabs. A comparison between the size of Jewish and Arab population along the line shows an amount of 290,000 Arabs as against 63,000 Jews, excluding the Jewish–Arab concentration in West and East Jerusalem, a conspicious advantage of 4.6 times in favour of the Arabs. The meaning of these basic deficiencies of the 'Green Line', which ought to secure Israel from terror in its sovereign territory, were herewith demonstrated. As mentioned, the line was not properly delineated, it remained physically broken because of twisted topography, it was impossible to close it hermetic, it has a large Arab population on both sides of it, and it lacks Jewish massive population which might block the accessibility of infiltraters or terrorists to Israel.

After the Six Day War there was a trend in Israel to disregard the existence of the 'Green Line' by the development of new settlements along it in order to erase its existence in the area. But nowadays the 'Green Line' came to life again because of the new political circumstances, as a vital importance to secure Israel, and as a borderline between Israel and the future autonomous area in Judea and Samaria. It seems that the 'Green Line' in its geographical and demographic conditions, is unable to promise too much, unless it will be fortified as a sofisticated and perfect security line, as in the northern Israeli–Lebanon security zone, as the line between Israel and Jordan, or as the borderline between Israel and Syria. Such a step to be taken by the Israeli government might be very expensive, and politically and economically not realistic, and what remains is, to speed up and accelerate the peace process with the Palestinians, so that the 'Green Line' will not be needed anymore as a security line against terror and sabotage.

Late Prime Minister Yitzhak Rabin declared in 1995 about the need to seperate between the Arab population in Judea and Samaria and the Jewish one in Israel, and appointed a committee of experts representing different Israeli security bodies to prepare a plan for a seperation line east of the former 'Green Line', but parallel to it, with all the needed installations to provide Israel's security. With this act Israel joined the countries which planned and constructed artificial seperation boderlines to protect their territorial and economic security. Artificial seperation lines with fences, watchtowers and walls are still frequent in many countries. The United States layed for many years with the idea of digging a system of deep and wide canals and trenches, in a total lenght of 3,520 kilometers between its territory and Mexico, in order to prevent unlegal infiltration of foreigners into her territory. Morocco built a high sandstone barrier, 2,480 kilometers long, along its desert fringe, in order to protect the West Sahara territory, the former Spanish Sahara, which she claimed for, and to stop the guerillas who penetrated into the area during years with the aim to achieve independence and sovereignty for West Sahara. South Africa built in 1980 an electronic fence whith barbed wire, that was installed along an important and strategic section between the country and Zimbabwe, in order to prevent the passage of people who were seeking for work or coming for sabotage. On the peninsula of Malesia a fencc 56 kilometers long was erected, with many watchtowers to protect the northern borderline with Thailand. Even the borderlines between Russia and Finnland or Russia and Turkey were known since ever as threathening borders, protected properly by the Russians with a system of fences and watchtowers. Seperation lines of conflicts will exist so long as territories and countries do exist, because regimes strive to achieve more space and sovereignty over land. At any time there are all over the world about a hundred of existing territorial conflicts between neighbouring countries, and problems of dominance and protection arise every now and then. The conflict between Israel and the Palestinians is one of the many that exist today.

It may be assumed, that the new seperation line which Israel intends to delineate in Judea and Samaria will not be able to close the border hermetically, because of the mountainous terrain and the strong interrelationships which exist between the territories and Israel regarding Israel's need for working manpower and the places of employment which the Arab population needs. Along the 'Green Line', as in many other closed and protected borderlines in the world, some 'grey' areas may be created. Since ever were these 'grey' areas fringe territories of sovereign space of countries, or countries in evolution. Their importance was almost always temporarily, they were passable for immigrants, workers and refugees, till they were totally abolished and became populated, stable and successive regions of countries.

An effective partition line cannot be achieved by a temporary and hurried delineation, as it is in the recent case of Israel, but only after a long time of an economic and demographic development on both sides of it. Boundaries have been delineated in many cases very rapidly because of political and military circumstances before the appropriate and effective means were prepared to make them function properly. It is doubtful whether seperation lines and artificial borders are able to prevent totally immigration of population from neighbouring countries which are economical unequal. The immigration of foreigners who escape from hunger and poverty and from political discrimination, cannot be stopped hermetically even with the most perfect means. The power of immigration of foreigners will not change even if better seperation lines will be erected. The only solution for that is the creation of steady and better economic conditions, and more places of employment for people, on both sides of them.

From the above demonstration some consequences may be drawn concerning Judea and Samaria. Only a fundamental economic solution in the territories, which will create more places of employment for the local population, will ensure the effectiveness of the seperation line between Israel and the Palestinians, and no barriers, closure periods, guarding posts, patrols, watchdogs and electronic fences will solve the existing political problem. The new seperation line between Israel and the Palestinians, which has been planned and waits for implementation, should not be closed hermetically, as that between Israel and Syria. It should be a temporary line to enable options for a final peace agreement on the borderlines revisions of the future Palestinian State, with the hope, that "good fences make good neighbours".

Urban Political Geography of Jerusalem

Few cities evoke such strong emotional response from so many people as does Jerusalem. Sacred to at least three major religions, Jerusalem has long been a source and a scene of contention among the adherents of these faiths and their political sponsors. During the past half of the 20th century, each of the three religions, represented by a Christian, a Jewish, and an Islamic polity, has attemped to determine the orientation of development in the city. Each effort has had only limited success. The particular physical characteristics of Jerusalem and the religious aspects of the settlement have produced a unique combination of factors that affect decisions by politicians and planners, regardless of the controlling administration. These conditions are likely to remain influental in the future.

Since 1948 Jerusalem has usually been discussed in terms of a threefold division: the Old City, East Jerusalem and West Jerusalem (Fig. 15). The Old City comprises five areas: the Armenian quarter, the Jewish quarter, the Moslem quarter, and the Temple Mount, which, depending on religious orientation, is also known as Mount Moriah, Dome of the Rock, or Haram esh–Sharif. The Old City is conveniently and precisely defined by its impressive encircling walls, built during the reign of the Turkish Sultan Suleiman the Magnificent early in the Sixteenth century.

East Jerusalem usually refers to the parts of the city outside the walls of the Old City that were under Jordanian rule between 1948 and 1967. The population of East Jerusalem is mostly Arab. West Jerusalem has been under Israeli control since 1948 and the population is predominantly Jewish (Efrat and Noble, 1988).

Site and Situation

The status and the importance of Jerusalem throughout the course of its long history have been determined partially by its location in the Judean hills at the intersection of north–south and east–west routes. The alignment of the north south passage between Samaria and Judea lies in fairly narrow limits, because any significant westward shift would place it against deep ravines and valleys that form the contact zone between the coastal plain and the hills. Farther eastward the route would abut a series of deep canyons along the face of a rift valley. Similarly an east–west route located farther northward would lead to the sterile desert in Samaria, and a southern displacement would lead to the sterile desert in Samaria, and a southern displacement is thwarted by the expanse of the Dead Sea. Only directly through Jerusalem does the route focus on the oasis of Jericho in the Jordan Valley.

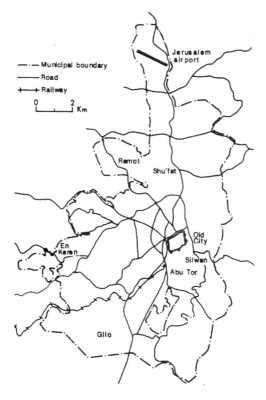

Fig. 15: The Area of Jerusalem   73

Although the broken nature of the plateau on which Jerusalem is located has been a factor in the city's becoming a central, nodal point and a stronghold dominating a wide area, the site is surrounded by even higher elevations. This location and the availability of local water supplies in ancient times explain both the choice of site and many aspects of the connection in recent history between Israeli and Jordanian forces.

In the 20th century the center of gravity for the city has oscillated with the changing political fortunes. At the beginning of the British Mandate (1919) the municipal boundary of Jerusalem encompassed an area of 12.7 square kilometers, 59 percent of which was the Old City. The influx of Jewish people during the Mandate period forced further extension of the boundaries, and the city–planning area reached 37.5 square kilometers by 1948. Between 1948 and 1967 the city was partitioned and its settled area was reduced in size because of political uncertainties. Eastward development since 1967 has been limited, although there has been expansion onto surrounding heights for strategic reasons.

The uneven topography of the Jerusalem region profoundly affects settlement and growth patterns of the city. Hillocks and isolated interfluves alternate with winding valleys and scattered basins. These lower–lying areas originally were used for agriculture and for access, and on the steeper slopes were wastelands, forested parks, cemeteries, and public open spaces. The high elevations became the locations of residential neighbourhoods and independent villages that were subsequently absorbed by the expanding city. The mosaic of residential clusters seperated by agricultural, open, or institutional zones emerged as the standard pattern of settlement in late 2Oth–century Jerusalem.

The long–established neighbourhoods beyond the Old City developed through years of accretion. Instead of displaying the conventions of modern city planning, they often reflect the personalities of their founders and original inhabitants who generally had a common origin and who formed a close–knit social group. In contrast with the modern practice of neighbourhoods or towns planned by central–governmental authority that are settled with heterogeneous inhabitants who must undergo social education to adapt to new surroundings and neighbours, these old communities began with residents of relatively similar background, experience, and orientation. Settlements of this type were associated with each major religion.

More than thirty such residential neighbourhoods had emerged in Jerusalem prior to World War 2. The Jewish settlements were mostly west of the Old City. A further impetus to the proliferation of distinctive residential neighbourhoods emerged solely in the Jewish community. Jews often refrain from mixing with their neighbours, a tradition thas reflected centuries of discrimination in widely scattered areas. Most Jews who arrived after 1918 were not as bound by the conservative religious traditions, and conflict and tension soon arose between orthodox and liberal groups. With continued population growth, crowding and congestion in the Jewish settlements eventually led to the planning and the erection of neighbourhoods in western architecture styles prevelant in the 1920s and the 1930s. However, the established neighbourhoods were largely unaffected by new trends. Gradually long–term residents who were less bound by conservative religious interpretations migrated into the westerly parts of the city, and the buildings thus evacuated in the old quarters were taken by the expanding orthodox Jewish communities.

The neighbourhoods of East Jerusalem are more likely than ones elsewhere to be outgrowths of independent villages that coalesced. These neighbourhoods tend to be traditional in orientation and unpatterned in layout. With other parts of the Muslim world they shared rigid ideas about neighbourhood form and housing to ensure maximum privacy of women and to deflect casual traffic from private spaces (Costa and Noble , 1986).

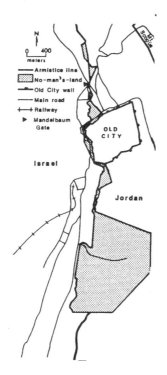

Fig. 16: The Armistice Line in Jerusalem 1948 - 1967

75

From 1948 to 1967 Jerusalem was a politically and a religiously divided city. The armistice line in 1949 confirmed the division of the city and created a neutral zone to be administered by the United Nations between the Jordanian and Israeli military positions (Fig. 16). That no man's land comprised seven areas, but along most of the dividing line, hostile positions were immediately adjacent to each other. The armistice line ran through land that was open, undeveloped, or occupied by former roadways. The Jordanian army occupied the Old City and East Jerusalem, and the Israeli army controlled Mount Zion, West Jerusalem, and an important enclave on Mount Scopus.

The division symbolized by the armistice line worsened during the next 19 years. Each political sector in the city underwent seperate development with different orientations. Connections between eastern and western Jerusalem were effectively severed, because streets were often blocked by cement walls as a protection against snipers, and prominent buildings near the line were fortified. In the central area, the Jordanians had the advantage of occupying the massive 16th–century walls.

The portion of Jerusalem under Israeli control was oriented to the narrow corridor connecting it with the rest of Israel ultimately the Mediterranean coast. Arab Jerusalem was generally focused eastward, especially toward Amman, the capital of Jordan. The population of the city was almost totally segregated on the basis of etnicity: virtually no Arabs, either Muslim or Christian, lived in West Jerusalem, and no Jews inhabited East Jerusalem. Immediately after the division, the occupants of the Jewish quarter in the Old City were forcibly evacuated to Jordan, but they were released nine months later. Most of the Arab residents in West Jerusalem fled at the outbreak of hostilities.

In 1948 and immediately thereafter, Israel authority in Jerusalem seemed to be better organized than the Jordanian counterpart. The former quickly recognized that effective claims had to be based on physical control. By December 1949, the Israeli government began to shift offices from Tel Aviv to Jerusalem, and on January 1950, the Knesset averred that the city has always been the Israeli capital. In many circles that move was considered to be a contravention of the U.N. resolutions that had decreed the international status of the city. Most foreign governments did not transfer their embasis from Tel Aviv to Jerusalem (Goodman, 1974) Nevertheless, Jerusalem has functioned as the de–facto capital since 1950.

The Arab sector of Jerusalem did not enjoy the level of organization and efficiency that characterized the Israeli portion. Part of the situation was the confused political circumstances that marked the fate of the Arab Palestinian territory and advocacy. The Arab state projected in the U.N. resolutions about postwar Palestine did not materialize, and the central Arab Zone was ultimately absorbed by Jordan. The political change implied an economic one. Under the British Mandate Jerusalem had been the commercial and economic center of Judea, Samaria and Trans–Jordan. The City linked that large region to the Mediterranean ports of Jaffa and Haifa. The absorption of the West Bank by Jordan also shifted the orientation of commercial activities eastward to Amman. Merchants in tbe Old City, previously wholesalers and suppliers for the East Bank, became dependent on imports from Amman.

The eastward orientation affected the physical layout of Arab Jerusalem and encouraged its spread eastward onto the difficult terrain of the Judean desert as well as along the road to Jericho and toward Ramallah on the north. Another highly significant aspect was the increased pressure to develop the eastern flanks of the Temple Mount, the Qidron Valley, and the Mount of Olives, areas whose use was especially sensitive because of their Jewish and Christian associations.

Expansion of Arab Jerusalem was also hampered by a general lack of suitable space for rapid urban development. Areas to the east and south–east not only opened archeological considerations, but had also unsuitable terrain for expansion. Little expansion occurred to the south, because the direct connection to Bethlehem had been severed. The winding roads subsequently built on the eastern flank of the Jerusalem hills was hardly an urban thoroughfare. Expansion was consquently channeled along the saddle in the hills, on both sides of the Jerusalem – Ramallah corridor on the north.

The Jewish–Arab Struggle for the Environs in Jerusalem.

The Six Day War began on 5 June 1967. Shortly after its conclusion, Israeli annexation of East Jerusalem and the Old City brought Jerusalem under a single political control. For security reasons, military officials and politicians made hasty decisions about the exact location of the new boundaries of the reunited city. Two goals guided those decisions: military considerations, especially the inclusion of heights to facilitate defence, and a desire to maximize the amount of territory but to minimize the size of the Arab population. Difficulties of achieving the latter were reflected in the fact that between 60,000 and 70,000 Arabs were included in the united city that was approximately three times larger in area than the exclusively Jewish pre–1967 portion controlled by Israel.

The new municipal boundary was drawn to include all the uninhabited no–man's–land and to incorporate areas of Mount Scopus on the north–east and the Mount of Evil consent and other heights on the south, so that a defensible perimeter existed in case of future conflict. The boundary was extended considerably to the north along the Ramallah road to encompass the airport, a military important site (Fig. 17).

Since the Six Day War unprecedented building activity has been conducted in the Jerusalem area with Arab financing and coordination betwen landowners, former mayors, heads of village councils and 'mukhtars'. Areas that were neglected were now cultivated, and every month dozens of houses were erected in the vicinity of the city.

The demand for workers from among the Arabs of the occupied territories grew in the course of time and the inhabitants of Judea, especially from Mount Hebron, began streaming to the building sites in Jerusalem, and gradually moved into the Old City of Jerusalem with their families, despite its crowded conditions. The original residents then moved into the Old City suburbs. The Arab population of Jerusalem has more than doubled itself since 1967, and now amounts about 160,000.

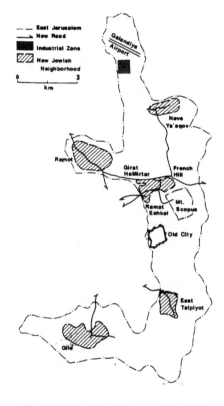

Fig. 17: Jewish and Arab Settlements in the Galileee

At the same time the demographic balance in the city has changed. The annual increase in the Jewish population was about half of the Arab and the ratio of 73.3 per cent Jews to 26.7 per cent Arabs in 1967 shifted to 72 percent Jews and 28 per cent Arabs in 1994. This trend has obtained since 1969, and figures have accelerated with the government–assisted move of Jerusalem residents to nearby towns beyond the 'Green Line'.

In recent years Arab construction in Jerusalem has also acquired a political tinge. The National Guidance Committee of the Arabs of the occupied territories has urged the inhabitants to plant trees and erect buildings in every place designated for Jewish settlement. The Arab villagers of Judea and Samaria made no distinction between State land and private land. For them both were Arab lands to which the occupation authorities had no right. The areas never operated according to an overall plan, had a long tradition of unauthorized building, and lack awareness of planning, so that the application of construction regulations there was extremely difficult (Efrat, 1988).

In the north–west villages of Jerusalem more than a thousand new buildings have been erected since 1967. On the mountainside north of Jerusalem more than 2,000 have been added in those years. East of Jerusalem the spread of Arab construction and the aquisition of land for building purposes was obvious. South of Jerusalem the pace of growth has been smaller, but there too amounts to several hundred units were added.

This accelerated Arab construction had implications for the future planning and development of Jerusalem. Some routes had to be changed due to these speedy Arab construction that interrupted the continuity of Israeli spread in many places. Arab construction had spatial and political implications, involving the occupation of considerable territory by a relatively small population, control of important roads connecting Jerusalem whith the environs, the placing of obstacles between sites of Jewish development, and the creation of difficulties in providing services.

These developments impelled the authorities to take preventive measures in the form of confiscating land. Jewish private individuals and public bodies have been acquiring hundreds of acres of land, occupying as much territory as possible in order to ensure orderly construction and development of the region in future. The settlement and development authorities claimed, that within one or two decades, the settlement policy of the government will prove to be a solution to the establishment of rural and semi–urban settlements, based on a comprehensive regional plan to the east of the Arab population. It will be effective and be able to compete in size with other Arab concentrations.

In regard to the Jewish areas of settlement in the region, in many places around Jerusalem Jewish settlements were erected. The townlet of Givat Zev, for instance, houses about 7,100 inhabitants. East of Jerusalem is the town of Maaleh Edummim, being rapidly populated and absorbed till 1995 about 16,000 inhabitants. The Jewish expansion over the region was designed to ensure control of access to Jerusalem, there being no desire to return to the pre–1967 situation, when Jerusalem was a cul–de–sac, cut off from its environs.

The Arab–Jewish struggle for the Jerusalem area has a demographic aspect as well. At the end of 1994 Jerusalem had about 552,000 inhabitants. The Jews numbered 393,000 (297,600 in 1981) and the non–Jews 159,000 (115,400 in 1981). Furthermore, the Jewish population of the city is aging, while the Arab population is becoming younger.

Twenty eight years of reunification, and eight years of the Arab uprising in Jerusalem, can be examined from the perspective of the functional interrelationship between Jews and Arabs, mainly in services and occupation (Romann, 1992).

As regards functions there are still two seperate cities in Jerusalem, inhabited by two different peoples, with two different religions, different cultures, different ways of life, and with different political orientations and aspirations. In more than a quarter of a century since 1967, no major Jewish business has shifted to the eastern section of the city, excluding the Jewish quarter of the Old City, and no Arab business moved to the Western Jerusalem. Arab workers, who reside in East Jerusalem, are employed by Jews in the western section, but no Jews are employed by Arabs. There are two systems of public transportation in the city, one Arab and one Jewish. A central Arab bus station is located in East Jerusalem, opposite Damascus Gate, while a Jewish one is located in the western section, without any functional connections between them. Health services, first aid stations and medical clinics exist seperately for Jews and for Arabs. Seperate restaurants, coffee–houses, cinemas and playhouses exist for Arabs in East Jerusalem and for the Jews in the western section. Arabic newspapers are printed and distributed only in East Jerusalem, while Hebrew ones circulate only in the western city.

Different systems of education function in Jerusalem. The Arab system is still based upon that established during Jordanian rule, while the Jewish system is based on Israeli governmental education programs. The Israeli government does not supervise any aspect of Arab education, nor provide any funding. Welfare and religious services are also seperate.

Despite considerable efforts made by the Israeli government and the municipality to create new and modern city facilities, the artificial reunification of the city has not been effective. The Arabs are not impressed with what has been achieved in the city during the last three decades, and they have expressed their attitude clearly by joining in the uprising. During the conflict the artificiality and basic weakness in the reunification of Jerusalem came as a great surprise to the Jewish leaders of the city. Former Mayor Teddy Kollek, often cited as a great unifying force in the face of divisions elsewhere, even had to admit that the delicate peaceful coexistence between the Jews and Arabs in Jerusalem had died.

Because of the uprising of the Arabs, Jerusalem has suddenly regressed many years. Along the seam line between East and West Jerusalem, where the armistice line and an open no–man's–land once divided the city into opposing sections, Arabs attack Jews with stones, and passing through the streets of East Jerusalem by Jews bacame dangerous. As a result, fewer Jews now visit the Western Wall in the Old City, and none enter the Dome of the Rock which has become a focus of Arab nationalism.

Without a declared war, and only after a relatively short time of unrest, the artificial fabric of unity was torn by demographic, geographic and politcal realities. Although Jerusalem has been decreed a reunified city, during the uprising it returned to its earlier status as a divided city, sundered along the so–called Gren Line'. The Israeli illusions of a Greater Jerusalem and a reunified city for the two peoples vanished, probably for ever.

These facts indicate, that the Jerusalem region is the site of a demographic and physical competition between two populations, aiming at substantive achievements with the clear political purpose of holding and controlling the environs of the city. It may be assumed that without a comprehensive political plan and rapid systematic implementation of important aspects of it, Israel will not be able to safeguard the region as a capital.

It may be assumed, that reunification of the city in 1967 did not bring an end to the divisions between Jews and Arabs. The animosities are deep and have survived the recent geographical shifts. Removal of political barriers among various parts of the city has demonstrated the influence of ephemeral circumstances on urban development between 1948 and the removal of artificially imposed barrier, operate throughout the municipal region, and have been able to demonstrate that they not only respond to events but also shape them.

The Jewish Qatif Bloc and the Gaza Strip

The decision of the Israel's government in 1995 to deploy its military forces from the Arab populated areas in the Gaza Strip, together with its policy of approving a Palestinian autonomy in "Gaza and Jericho first", arises among other things the problem of the remained Jewish settlements in the southern part of the Gaza Strip, which are included in the so–called "Qatif Bloc", and their future in the light of the new political situation which was created in this area.

The Qatif Bloc is an Israeli settlement area, designed to be a wedge between the Egyptian border at Sinai and the dense Arab population of the Strip, to maintain an Israeli presence in that sector of the occupied territories, and to establish Jewish settlements in a region whose political destiny has not full determined. It is a settlement bloc established adjacent to an enormous Arab population, grappling with problems of insufficient water and land, which due to its physical and geographical conditions, does not enable Jewish settlement on its territory. The settlement of the region was undertaken by Israel for security and political reasons, and a great deal of money was invested in it during years. The many attacks from the Palestinian 'Hamas' extremists on Jewish settlers and Israeli soldiers, which occured lately in the Bloc, and especially those that happened near the villages of Netzarim and Kefar Darom, and which caused many losts of soldiers' and citizens' lives, arise the question about the justification of continuous occupation of this bloc by Israel.

The Qatif Bloc includes actually twelve settlements, seperated into two groups. The northern part is the oldest, and includes Kefar Darom, Netzer Hazani, Qatif, and Gane Tal, while the more recently settled in the southern part include Neve Deqalim, Gedid, Gan Or, Bedolah, Morag, Bene Atzmon and others. In the center of the Strip, and very isolated, is the village of Netzarim, and in the northern corner of the Strip, very close to the Israeli borderline – three other settlements: Dugit, Nisanit and Elei Sinai. Settlement in the Bloc began in 1970 when a 'Nahal' army unit, combining security and military training with agricultural work, resettled Qefar Darom, which had been in existence before the War of Independence (1948). In 1972 other units settled Netzarim and Morag. In 1975 interest was reawakened in the settlement of the Strip, and land in the Qatif Bloc was handed over to a religious 'Moshav' federation, and many other settlements, mostly 'moshavim', based on personal cooperation in agriculture, were established.

The gatif Bloc occupies about 14,000 acres of land in the south–western part of the Gaza Strip. It is located on State land which before 1967 was controlled by the Egyptian army. The Bloc has no particular locational advantages. It was placed where there was unoccupied land that could be settled after basic reclaimation. From an Israeli security point of view its virtue is that it creates a seperation between Arab settlements, restricting their urban and agricultural expansion.

The Qatif Bloc is in fact an example of the establishment of an independent religious settlement region beyond the 'Green Line' to serve religious settlements. The Bloc faces a large number of problems, such as an insufficiency in land and water, while Arab population in the region is multiplying rapidly and needs land and water by itself. The dependence of the Bloc on means of production from outside, naturally reduces its ability to exist independently. The economic basis of the Bloc is not very stable either. Agriculture and tourism are the main economic sectors, while the Bloc is not favourable placed for industrial plants. It appears, that the establishment of a settlement bloc for geopolitical reasons does not always mean economic success, as proved in this case.

After Israel's deployment from the Arab cities and villages in the Gaza Strip in 1995, the Qatif Bloc remained as an enclave of Israeli settlements at the south–western corner of the Strip, excluding four other settlements which are located in the center and northern part of the Gaza Strip. After approving autonomy to the Arab part of the Gaza Strip, the functions and destinations of the Qatif Bloc remain unclear. No reasonable argument was yet declared by any official body regarding the importance of the Bloc today to Israel's security. Once its importance laid, as said, as a buffer zone between the Egyptian borderline and the dense Arab population which lives in the central part of the Strip, and as a region of concentrated Jewish settlements in an occupied area, but after the decision which was taken by the Israelis to withdraw from the Strip, what benefit can Israel derive from the existing Qatif Bloc in its present form, unless its destination is to function as a bargain card towards the negotiations with the Palestinians on the future of the occupied territories?

Although the valueable importance which right–wing politicians relate to the Qatif Bloc, that region is characterized by features which it really does not have: it has no adorned Jewish history behind it, and it is not a patrimony; most Israelis even don't have any special emotional relationship to this sandy corner in the southern part of the coastal plain; with its 5,300 inhabitants, it even has no demographic weight as against the 800,000 Arabs who live in the Gaza Strip; the Bloc is not so important in its agricultural production, and not even comparatively to the relative high production of the Arab rural population; it has no economic and social relations with the adjacent Besor Region and with other surrounding communities in Israel's territory; and its spatial and security importance opposite to the Egyptian borderline in Sinai is not great, as a result of the existing peace between the two countries.

The area of 14,000 acres which belong to the Bloc, encompassing 15 per cent of the total area of the Gaza Strip, and with its 16 settlements, endangers the Israeli soldiers, who are obliged to secure it, creates a logistic difficult problem to the military forces, which have to protect the settlers, to spread at the same time their troops behind long barbed wire lines and concrete cubes, and to secure the transportation of the settlers along twisted and dangerous arteries, with an invalueable cost of wasted money, energy and manpower. The reaction of the Israeli public to the deployment from the Gaza Strip, which was quite positive, indicates to a certain extent the need and justification of deployment from the Bloc either. Except the right–wing and religious circles' attitude in Israel to this region, as a part of a messianic conception to the Greater Land of Israel, no special interest could be found in the public toward these settlements, especially not with the athmosphere of evacuation which prevailes among the settlers, who envisage a high probabilty of withdrawal, which will soon or late occur, promising them big amounts of money as evacuation compensation.

It seems that a fundamental step has to be taken by the government in order to seperate between Jews and Arabs in this problematic region, which means actually, to transfer the whole Bloc to somewhere else. The late political settlement history in Israel reveales, that alternatives to settlement regions were found when it was necessary. The evacuation of the Yamit Region in northern Sinai, at the beginning of the 1980s, included a similar number of settlers as those of the Bloc. When the evacuation was decided on, the agricultural settlements were offered a substitute in a region, very similar to the Yamit area, regarding climate, soil, arid landscape, accessibility to main roads, development of economic and service branches, and even to establish a new–planned layout of settlements in the same system as they had, in the Shalom Region in the north–western Negev. The new settlements which were built in the Shalom Region were based on the same sources of livelihood and were a kind of copy of what existed on the other side of the border. The Shalom Region absorbed half of the families from Yamit Region, and this was viewed as a success. Settlements as Holit, Sufa and Talme Yosef even kept their previous names. If nowadays new urban settlements, as Eron in the northern part of the country, and Elad–Mazor in the central part, are being built, among others, for expected evacuees of Judea and Samaria, there is no reason why not to prepare reclaimed land for the Qatif Bloc inhabitants (Fig. 18).

Fig. 18: The Qatif Bloc and ist Surroundings

If to apply the evacuation model of the Yamit Region to the Qatif Bloc, with the assumption that most of the settlers will continue to be engaged in agriculture, and with the assumption that they will prefer to stay in the north–western Negev in the limits of a religious bloc of settlements, it will be possible to establish for them a new rural system of villages in the western Negev, on an open landscape which belongs now to the regional council of Eshkol, which cries for new settlers to come, and for more development, infrastructure, factories and public institutions. Even the filling–up of some of the existing settlements in the western Negev along the 'Green Line' is still actual and a possible solution, and the Jewish Agency, which is in charge of the establishment of rural setlements in the country, has prepared plans for the evacuees' resettlement. The many of the existing settlements, which are close to the borderlines of the Arab autonomous region along the Gaza Strip, need additional settlers, and so – the inner hinterland between Halutza in the south and the Lakhish Region in the north. If the settlers of the Qatif Bloc are really longing for the redemption of the Land of Israel for the People of Israel, it seems, that the western Negev might be the best place for them for carrying out their dreams.

The Future of the Golan Heights

The last declaration of Israeli's late Prime Minister Yitzhak Rabin about the political need of a minimal limited withdrawal in the Golan Heights, without enrooting anv settlement there, in condition that the Syrians will have to make a parallel step to the establishment of mutual diplomatic relations, was a dramatic step in Israel's policy. It arises naturally some basic questions: should Israel principally withdraw from the Golan Heights, and if so, till where should the withdrawal be without creating a meaningful change in Israel's strategic position in this area, and without justifying a revolt which the settlers of the Golan Heights are ready to organize in case such a step will be taken by the government.

Israel was always sensitive in regard to the Golan Heights, because Syria posed a threat before 1967 to the settlements of the Hula Valley and the Galilee below, and also because of the danger that the Syrians might divert the water of the Banias River and prevent the flow of water to the Jordan, which is Israel's principal water source. The conquest of the Golan Heights in the Six Day War removed the Syrian's threat, and for the first time created a substantial distance between Israel's northern settlements and Syria. The strategic advantage gained through the conquest of the Golan Heights may explain the speed with which Israel took steps to settle the conquered region, and the fear which exists nowadays to agree to any uncertain withdrawal from this region.

Jewish Settlement in the Golan Heights

After the Six Day War the various settlement institutions in Israel got together to work out a plan for the settlement of the Golan Heights. Wishing to put their political views into practice, they have applied the 'faits accompli' method in the region in order to force the hand of the government and the public, by acceleration settlement at Israel's northeastern border, thus obviating any possibility of withdrawal.

The planning and building of the settlements in the Heights was quite difficult, because on one hand the area had to be settled, and on other hand it could add very little to the Israeli economy in view of the needed investment in infrastructure. The inability to populate the center of the region was likewise a disadvantage, because not much could be done with uncultivable land.

But during the first years after the Six Day War, 11 agricultural settlements were established on the Golan Heights, some of them by 'Nahal' units. To begin with the settlement had a rather temporary character because there was little confidence regarding the future of the region. The government was being politically cautious, hesitant in regard to chances of success, and had only minimal impact on occurrences on the Golan Heights. However, the population in the Golan had gradually consolidated, and later it became more varied. In the course of the settlement endeavour the principle of location along the border came to be adopted. It was then that start was made in establishing blocs of three or four settlements with ten to twenty kilometers between the blocs. Most were in the south, fewer in the north, with a gap in the center.

The Yom Kippur War in 1973 caused great destruction on the Golan and cast doubt on the strategic capacity of the region. Some of the settlements were abandoned, and the defence status of the Golan Heights as a border region was considerably reduced. The Israeli government's conclusion from the war was, that the Golan Heights needed to be better fortified. It believed that despite what had happened to civilian settlement, was the best solution for security problems, and revealed great sensitivity regarding the center of the Hights, which remained vulnerable bare.

During the 1973–War the Syrians had pushed through to the heart of the Heights where there were no settlements. Consequently the Golan Heights center was now settled in three sections: a forward line of semi–rural settlements opposite the Syrian townlet Quneitra; two additional settlements in the south; and one more in the north between Quneitra and Mount Hermon.

In the middle of the 1970s it was decided, that in the empty spaces of the central Golan Heights, industrial villages and an urban center should be established. It is quite possible that had it not been for the unfavourable outcome of the Yom Kippur War (1973), this settlement endeavour in the central Golan Heights would never been initiated. The planning was done under the pressure of the geopolitical situation of the Golan Heights. The Yom Kippur War was certainly a critical turning point with regard to the development of the region, particularly in its center.

Between 1977–1987 the population of the Golan Heights arose from 2,200 to 6,500, and the number of settlements reached 31. The urban center of Qatzrin was developed and populated rapidly, and soon became the largest concentration of population in the Heights, with an economy based on light industry (Fig. 19).

The residents of the Golan Heights placed great hopes on the extension of Israeli law to their region, believing that such a step would provide the impetus for its accelerated development. But they proved to be mistaken. After the confirmation of the law in December 1981 the pace of development slowed. Only 6,500 Jews live in the settlements, about half the number of the Druze in the area, and another 3,000 in the townlet of Oatzrin.

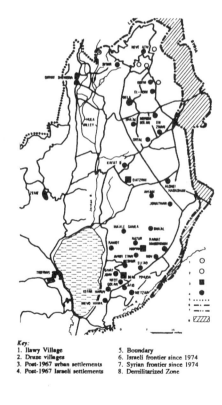

Key:
1. Ilawy Village
2. Druze villages
3. Post-1967 urban settlements
4. Post-1967 Israeli settlements
5. Boundary
6. Israeli frontier since 1974
7. Syrian frontier since 1974
8. Demilitarized Zone

Fig. 19: Settlements in the Golan Heights

From the geopolitical viewpoint the Golan Heights is an arena in which events are characterizable as follows: conquest for the purpose of acceleterated security settlement and defence; pressure for land for settlements with political motives and for cultivation; regional planning in order to integrate into the existing settlement complex in the Galilee; setting quite exaggerated population goals in a region of strategic importance; organizing settlement along lines paralleling the Syrian border, and in blocs; intensification in developing and populating the region as a result of the shock of the Yom Kippur War; and initial hesitation about continued settlement and later succumbing to public pressure to the point of extending Israeli law to the Golan Heights.

The Problem of Withdrawal

If we assume, that according to the late Prime Minister's declaration, no settlement indeed will be evacuated in the Golan Heights, and the whole problem applies only to a small withdrawal of only a few kilometers, without Israel's need to give up any rights and important properties, so then the margin of spatial possibilities for withdrawal remains anyhow very limited. A very careful examination of the geographical map of the Golan Heights indicates, that the number of sections where no withdrawal, from Israel's point of view, is logically, are higher than those which enable it to do so. It is illogical to withdraw, for instance, from the south–east of the Heights opposite to Hamat Gader and parallel to the Yarmuq River, because the negotiations between Israel and Jordan regarding the division of the rivers' water are continuing. There will not be any space at the present situation for a withdrawal along the Ruqad River, opposite to the southern Jewish settlements of the Golan, along the Nevo-Ramat Magshimim axis, because they are situated in a Hama distance of only 2–5 kilometers from the Syrian frontier line. There is also no logical reason for a partial withdrawal along the Ramat Magshimim – Alone Ha–Bashan – En Zivan axis, because of the topographical importance of this section opposite to the Syrian territory, wich includes relative high mountains as Mounts Peres, Josifon and Shifon, and the more so, that opposite to them run the narrow parallel seperation lines between Israel and Syria established in 1974, with only a few meters between them. There is also no possibility at present for a withdrawal opposite to the demilitarized townlet of Quneitra which belongs to Syria, because may be that at some time it will be resettled by Syrian inhabitants who may create an increasing threatening concentration of population opposite to the Jewish settlements of En Zivan and Merom Ha–Golan, which are situated very close to the border. Even along the northern border of the Golan Heights, not enough space for any withdrawal is nowadays to be found, because of the Israeli important strategic points of

Mounts Hermon and Dov, known as „the eyes of Israel opposite to the Damascus plain", and also because of the high importance of some other mountains, as Kahal, Betarim and some topsites which are located about 1,500 meters high. Even not the surroundings of the bisected Druze village Agar could be taken into account for withdrawal, because of the importance of the Snir River's water which flows nearby to Israel.

After a topographical, strategic and settlement elimination of the area, what remains for any further step is only one section in north–east of the Golan Heights which may be a target for a limited spatial withdrawal. That is the section between Quneitra and the Druze village of Majdal Shams, which also includes the Druze villages of Buqata and Masade. This section, east of Mountains Varda and Ram, is 15 kilometers long and 4–5 kilometers wide, and is dominated by higher topographical points in the west, as Mounts Hermonit and Odem. May be, that the giving–up of this section, where 2–3 Druze villages with strong nationalistic, social and cultural relationships to Syria remained, might be a relative easy solution, with no meaningful danger to Israel from the small Syrian villages opposite to it.

If that will the potential area for Israel's first small and symbolic withdrawal from the Golan Heights to examine Syrian's seriousness and readiness to negotiate with Israel toward the achievement of a peace agreement, may be that there is no reason for the present demonstrations that are held now in Israel by the Golan settlers against withdrawal, and perhaps there should also be are any no objective reason for the angry responses of the public when the whole discussion will concentrate on a small section which comprises not more than 75 square kilometers or 6.5 per cent of the Golan Heights. Excluding the principal position of no withdrawal from the Golan Heights and its political meaning to Israel, which is totally expressed by the Golan settlers, symbolic withdrawal is worthwile to may be that a small achieve a further political step which may lead to a peace treaty between Israel and Syria.

Israel's Water Problems

More than five million inhabitants of Israel and about two million of Palestinians suffer already from lack of water in Israel. It is supposed, that when Israel's population will reach eight million in the year 2020, and the Palestinians three million, the shortage of water will be even worse. For each available cubic meter of water there will be a lack of another one. The consumption of water will then be about four milliard cubic meters annually, but in the pipelines only two milliard cubic meters of water will flow.

Three factors cause usually the shortage of water in countries all over the world: rapid increase of population, unequal distribution of water resources, and the using–up of water faster then it can be replenished. The common reason for international disputes is usually water resources. There are at least two regions in the world where a political conflict arose lately because of dams building. A political dispute exists between Slovakia and Hungary because of Hungarian's objection to the building of a dam on the Danube River by the Slovaks, a project which may cause besides its ecological damage, a shortage of water in Hungary. A similar situation exists in the Euphrates river basin. Repeated suggestions for cooperative water management have failed to bring Turkey, Syria and Iraq together in this issue. These three heavily armed states came to the brink of confrontation, when Turkey shut off the flow of the Euphrates in order to fill its new Attaturk Dam, a part of a sweeping project to make 120,000 square kilometers of land arable. A similar conflict is brewing between Egypt and Ethiopia over the headwaters of the Nile.

Water in the Middle East

Water has been a touchy geopolitical issue in the Middle East. Israel faces a steadily worsening water shortfall and its neighbours face even worse. The issue is more sensitive than ever. In the absence of any significant likelihood that peace will turn the distribution of water into a simple business transaction, there is an ever increasing possibility that force may be used to determine who has water and who is to be deprived of it.

Israel is currently estimated to be using up its water resources 15 percent faster than they can be replenished. Israel, Jordan and Egypt are expected to reach a 30 percent water deficit by the end of the decade, while Syria and Iraq are expecting a gap of 60 percent by then. Despite the risk of war over water, little is being done in the region to increase the efficiency of water use, or even to utilize all existing sources. Distribution in Arab countries for both farming and domestic use is behind the times. At the same time, water from under–exploited rivers in Turkey pours uselessly into the Mediterranean, because Turkey's offers to pipe it to its neighbours have been rejected for political reasons. As in so many cases in the Middle East, the degree of rationality with which a problem is addressed is in inverse proportion to its importance. Most Arab reactions to the possibility of cooperating with Israel on development of water resources have been nothing short of suicidal.

Water Disputes in Israel

As the Ottoman Empire crumbled after the World War 1, the location of water resources, particularly the headwaters of the Jordan River, influenced the boundaries of the French and British Mandates, later – the borders between Israel, Lebanon, Syria and Jordan (Wolf, 1995). As the population in Palestine grew in the 1930s and the 1940s against hydrologic limits, so grew the dangers of conflict over water. In those years water was a focus of several reports that tried to determine the economic absorbtive capacity land. These reports influenced British, Arab, and Jewish attitudes and policies towards immigration and land settlement. After the establishment of the State of Israel in 1948 armed conflicts between Syria and Israel occurred concerning the water resources on the upper Jordan River. American intervention in the middle of the 1950s through the mediator Eric Johnson was carried on to reach a water–sharing agreement between the riparians of the Jordan River. Although unrastified for political reasons, the allocations agreed to by Arab and Israeli technical committees have generally held with recognized modifications. With technical Israeli and Jordanian representatives these talks have proved fruitful over the years in reducing minor tensions around the Jordan and Yarmuq Rivers. With the Arab decision in the middle of the 1960s to build an Al–Arab diversion of the Jordan headwaters to preclude the Israeli Water Carrier, and ending when Isreali tanks and air strikes halted construction on the diversion, this was then a period of the most direct water related conflict (Wolf, op. cit.).

The Six Day War changed regional reparian positioning. Israel aquired two of the three Jordan River headwaters, riparian access to the entire river and the recharge zone for mountain aquifers that currently supplies about 40 percent of Israel's water supply. Since 1967 ownership and management conflicts occurred between Israel and the Palestinians in the occupied territories of Judea, Samaria and the Gaza Strip, and between Israel and the Jordanians and the Syrians. Since 1991 an impetus towards cooperation grows as regional talks develop, and final solutions have been agreed upon between Israel and Jordan by signing a peace treaty through which Jordanian gained an addition of water supply from the Israeli water reservoir of Lake Kinneret.

The war on the water resources in the Middle East remained ever since without basic agreements. The dominance on the West Bank water, for instance, is one of the most delicate issues in the negotiations on the peace process between Israel and the Palestinians. The West Bank includes about 40 percent of Israel's underground water in aquifers which at the same time also supplies 90 percent of the consumption of the Arab population. Israel dominates all the water resources in Judea and Samaria, but the Palestinians claim that only 17 percent of these resources are allowed to be used by them. Israel claims on other hand that while this underground water runs into her territory she has the right to use it according to her needs, precedently to the water exploitation before the Six Day War.

Israel drilled 30 new wells in Judea and Samaria, but their water is used by the Israeli settlers only, while the Palestinians were not allowed to drill new wells for themselves. As a result the Arab farmers suffered from the Israeli settlers' deep–pumping which dried up their wells. In the present situation, each benefit in water to one population is on the account of the other. Without creating new resources of water together with equal and proportional distribution, the conflict in the area will remain unsolved. New resources could be created by circulation of drainage water, by introducing advanced methods in agriculture which will decrease water consumption, as the development of crops that withstand salty irrigation water.

Israel's special water problem lies in the urgent need to recycle sewerage water which is getting during the years more salty and polluted. Israel and the Palestinians should therefore invest all their knowledge and energy in purification of sewerage water, so that the water problem for agriculture will be less strict. As water specialists estimate, an investment of 550 million dollar for a purification plan of sewerage water in the area till 2010 might add 870 million cubic meters to the potential water resources for Israel and the Palestinians. By both peoples the demand for water is much higher than the bid. In the Israeli urban and industrial sectors the average demand is 100 cubic meters per person per year, as against 35 in the West Bank and the Gaza Strip. In the next few decades the Palestinian's demand for water will increase and became equal to that of the Israelis. The present water resources in Israel, including the underground water, the Jordan basin catchment area, flood water and the recycled water, provide about two million cubic meters annually, which is not enough for future consumption. These resources will not increase their amounts of water significantly, so that other artificial and sophisticated methods should be introduced.

A basic solution for additional resource of water in Israel, mainly for the urban sector, could be water desalinization. The cost of one cubic meter today is about one dollar, but it may, according to spacialists' estimations, be decreased to 75–80 cent. Also a practical project for Israel might be the digging of three canals: one from the Gulf of Elat to the Dead Sea; one from the Mediterranean to the Dead Sea; and one from the Mediterranean to the Galilee in order to increase the flow of sea water through the country. These projects may increase the creation of desalinated water at certain sites with the waterfall energy, and improve the landscape around them.

As far as the water problems of Israel and its occupied territories are discussed, a strict division of the water between the peoples concerned may be a bad solution, because all the neighbouring countries rely on the same underground water resources in the region. If one country pollutes these resources, all the other consumers will loose their water. In this aspect Israel and the Palestinians may be compared to two beggars who have to share between them not more than nothing. After the peace treaty which has been signed with Jordan, and the bi–lateral negotiations with the Palestinians which are held nowadays, all parties have to unite in order to find a common solution for the increase of water potential in this area. Appropriate sites for desalinization plants may be found at the Mediterranean or at the Red Sea coastlines. Division of water means further conflicts in the future, and when the parties will realize that alternative resources could be created in a scientific and technological way, the water problem in Israel and its neighbouring countries will not be anymore a threat for the whole region.

The Policy of Regional Development

Israel has an experience of about 50 years in regional development. Its geographic and demographic background raised conflicting situations for regional planners, politicians and developers. Rapid developing was carried out in Israel since 1949 according to governmental guidelines which stressed the policy of ingathering the Jewish exile and provision of all the needed facilities for immigrants. Regional development succeeded mainly in the establishing of more than 30 new towns for the immigrants, in reducing of the population in the metropolitan areas and in the dispersion of population to peripheral regions in the country. Recent changes in regional development tend to concentrate on detailed regional planning and development according to the future political situation following the gradual solving of the Israeli–Palestinian conflict in the occupied territories.

Geographical Background of Regional Development

The State of Israel provided a good opportunity for professional development, both on the regional scale, as well as for more detailed development. Geographical conditions on one hand, and rapid economic and demographic changes on the other, created a great challenge for developers, who had to work to solve problems in unsettled circumstances. Although Israel's experience in development is mere 50 years, but nevertheless, it is full of dynamism and modifications in aims and objectives.

Israel is a small country, which before the Six Day War (1967) extended over an area of about 20,700 square kilometers. Since 1967 it had to qovern administered areas in Judea, Samaria, excluding Jericho, and a small part in the southern Gaza Strip. Although the State of Israel is small, it displays many geographical contrasts:
- a Mediterranean climate in the north and an arid one in the south, seperated by a distance of only 250 kilometers.
- abundant precipitation in the north with a surplus of water, and very little rainfall in the Negev in the south which is virtually unpopulated.
- alluvial and fertile soils along the coastal plain with a high potential for agriculture; however in this area, there is continuous pressure to build houses, settlements and roads and to accomodate many other non–agricultural activities.

- minerals such as phosphates and potash are to be found in the southern part of the country, while the industrial centers are mainly in the north, spread over a relatively large area.
- almost half of Israel's population is concentrated and congested along the coastal plain, while the mountainous regions of Galilee, Judea and the Negev remain sparcely populated.

To this may be added the fact, that the Jewish population is very heterogeneous; it grew through waves of immigration since 1948. The people came from 70 countries with different cultural backgrounds, dissimilar languages, and myriad ways of life, habits and manners.

The geographic and demographic background of the State, therefore, raised conflicting situations, which the regional developers had to tackle. for example, the encouragement of population to live in semi–arid and mountainous regions, as opposed to the natural trends of the Israelis and new immigrants alike to concentrate in the big cities; the development of agriculture in the hill–country, as opposed to the trend of the farmers to cultivate soil along the coastal plain and in inner valleys; the development of new planned urban centers and modern housing, as opposed to old and unplanned nuclei and centers in veteran villages and towns; the aspiration of planners to develop more industrial sites and agricultural regions, as opposed to the lack of arable agricultural soil and available minerals; the development of a modern country with integrated economy, as opposed to the close borderlines between Israel and the neighbouring states and the country's isolation in the Middle East.

These conflicting problems and many others in the political and economic field became a real challenge to regional developers. Their ultimate task was to develop a new–born country, with many needs and which found itself under pressure of serious daily problems of security.

The Aims and Effects of Regional Development

Regional development in Israel began in 1949. The rapid development of almost every physical object in the country, and the growing needs, sometimes made basic research and survey impossible. Therefore, the government outlined a policy for regional development according to which many projects have been executed (Dash & Efrat, 1964). The most important points of this policy were:

the right for every Jew to immigrate to Israel and to receive all the facilities required for living and for work.
- the dispersion of the population throughout the country with priority being given to undeveloped regions. The underlying reasons were security problems and to prevent

94

the congestion of the population on a small part of the country, mainly in the Tel Aviv region, which could make development and housing impossible.

- the preservation of agricultural land for agricultural uses only and the development of housing projects on non agricultural land. Preservation was very crucial because agricultural land is very sparse, extending mainly along the coastal plain, where it competes with the concentration of population and the growth of housing projects.

- economic priority, by means of investments, to peripheral towns and regions in order to populate them rapidly and make them attractive for further investment and development.

- economic priority for Jerusalem in order to strengthen the capital of Israel economically. This was needed because Jerusalem is located in a mountainous area which is difficult to develop and because the capital is quite remote from the urban centers in the coastal plain.

- developing and building of a hierarchy of urban centers which differ in size and economic functions. The purpose was to disperse functions all over the country, even to smaller towns, and to prevent the whole economy of the country from being dependent upon a few urban centers.

- the encouragement of the agricultural sector as a whole in order to secure food poduction as much as possible.

- intensification of industry in the new towns to provide an economic basis so that new immigrants can live in them.

- easy access to every settlement in the country within a functional network of roads.

- the preservation of the natural beauty of the country and its historic sites which are in danger of destruction with the intensive developmemt of housing presently taking place.

- the preservation of the coastline for recreational purposes only. The idea behind it was that the seashore has to be free for every citizen in the country as a permanent source of recreation.

On the basis of these directives, a great deal has been achieved in the country: comprehensive development plans for regions and districts were prepared; these laid down the blueprint for the construction of roads, railways, airports, national parks for more than 30 new towns, location for industry, agricultural zones, new villages, urban satellites etc.

As a result of this planning and development the percent of population within the three metropolitan areas has declined from 54% of the total in 1948 to 40% in 1994, and the share of the Tel Aviv metropolitan area in the Jewish population of the country fell from 40.5% in 1948 to 28.8% in 1994. The three major agglomerations increased, however, in absolute numbers, but growth was checked and kept below the average for the country as a whole.

Many of the new towns in Israel have contributed to the stabilization of rural districts. They function as reservoires of manpower – unskilled and skilled employees in agriculture, industry and construction. All the towns have received investment for industrial plants and together with direction of manpower. Many new industries have flourished. New towns such as Ashdod, Elat and Ashqelon are becoming urban centers and service centers for their regions, while a few others, like Qiryat Gat, Arad and Karmiel have even developed typical economic functions.

Most of the agricultural land has been preserved for agricultural uses, and urban development in these areas was prevented. New harbours such as Elat and Ashdod were built; also a network of roads and highways were constructed. Jerusalem was replanned and built–up as a modern capital; many other towns, such as Beer Sheba, Ashqelon, Nazareth Illit, Acre and Tiberias had sections which were redeveloped; and many veteran settlements developed into towns. Much has been done in the preservation of the landscape, antiquities, areas of natural beauty and of the shorelines. Numerous new hotels were erected, and the whole field of tourism found itself in high priority of development in parts of the country.

The New Development Trends

The regional development policy of the first period of the State of Israel was pursued with considerable energy and obstinacy, but lacked consistency and coordination. It has achieved certain remarkably successes and at the same time suffered serious setbacks. In trying to uncover the roots of these setbacks, we have to point out the conservative character of this policy in its aspiration (Brutzkus, 1970). Because of the background of the first planning arrivals to Israel, who left the exile in Eastern Europe, their ideology was against urbanization, against modern housing, against private transportation and against many other spontaneous trends of a modern country. For example, the initiators of this policy assumed that agriculture would absorb more than 20% of the population. This figure has already dropped to 4 in 1995.

A further basic assumption was that the existing anti urban attitude of collective and cooperative settlements would gradually disappear and give place to far–reaching cooperation between the new regional urban centers and the rural hinterland. This was too optimistic. Ideological barriers remained and the rural councils, guided mainly by veteran kibbutzim (cooperative settlements), continued their traditional anti–urban attitude. They remained, on the whole, indifferent to the fate of the new urban centers and aimed to reduce the social, cultural, and even economic contacts with them. The direct link between the rural settlement and the major cities was reduced as motorization grew. Now the new urban centers bypass the agricultural settlements and function with the large cities instead.

The change in the extent and composition of Jewish immigration and their reluctance to be directed to development areas also made the replacement of population losses in the development towns, caused by backflows to the coastal plain, more and more difficult. Poor architectural design and very low housing standards did not contribute to the efficiency or attractiveness of the development towns. Low densities in the early stages, and high multi–storey apartment blocks today, make the whole physical environment poor and dull. There was also some exaggeration in applying theories of hierarchial settlements in this small country, and instead of erecting so many new towns in a short time, it would have been better to erect a few, but on a larger scale. The many new towns did not always develop together with sources of employment, thus causing emigration to the metropolitan areas. Regional development was not always worked out in detail and according to stages of execution and budget. It was not always based upon economic decisions, and there was generally a difference in the projected periods of these plans – the difference being that economic plans were short–range while the development plans were long–range.

At the beginning of the State's development, integration of new immigrants, which was held as one of the basic ideas in social and physical planning, was not as easy as thought previously, and sometimes veteran population and the newcomers and between the immigrants themselves, because of their heterogeneous character. This had an effect upon the standard of agricultural settlements and upon the infrastucture of service centers.

In the 1970s regional development as a whole was laid down and crystallized new aims and trends appeared. On the basis of what was done before, detailed development became very important. Also comprehensive development with an emphasis on economics, sociology, geography and administration is increasingly used today. In regional development, the construction of a main road is no longer as important, as the building of bridges and junctions; not the siting of a new town as the improvement of an existing town's infrastucture; not the limiting of a national park as the detailed developing of it for all kinds of recreational uses; not only the preservation of agricultural land as the planning of its best economic uses.

The field of regional development today has therefore widened considerably, in particular it includes the detailed development of urban agglomerations and that of Tel Aviv proper; also the development of industrial zones; local development of harbours; detailed development of institutions according to economic and social functions of cities; development of multi–storey apartment houes, and development of modern transportation and communications systems.

The State of Israel has undergone many changes whithin a short time. If we consider the characteristics of the development projects executed, rather than the scale of these projects, we may say, that Israel's development problems today are similar to those of European developed countries.

We may find in Israel the same international problems of a desire to raise the standard of living; we find a growing number of private cars using the highways; a trend to develop suburban settlements with a high standard of construction; an immense growth of urban centers along the coastal plain; ribbon development along the main roads; a growing service sector; a growing number of national and regional institutions which are also a result of the higher standard of living; a continuous improvement in housing, an emigration of population from agricultural areas to metropolitan areas; and a congestion of the population along the coastal plain. All these are features which characterize modern countries.

The big countries of the world struggle with these problems of development. In Israel the struggle is much harder because of the additional struggle for security and peace, and the current political problem which exists, concerning the solution which has to be found in order to achieve peace in the region.

The Galilee as a Political Conflict between Jews and Arabs

The Galilee in the northen part of Israel exemplifies the struggle between two peoples for land, for settlement and livelihood, and for the prevention of further demographic increase by the other one. The Jews are especially interested in this region to preserve governmental–owned land in order to ensure their settlement existence in the future. The Israeli way to achieve this goal lies in what is called the "Judaizing of the Galilee". The chances for Jewish population and settlement increase, comparing to the development and construction in the last four decades in the Galilee, should therefore be examined according to the following aspects: the settlement history in the region; the geographical reality that existed before 1948; the development and settlement activities executed by the Israelis after the establishment of the State; and the means which Israel own for further investment and development in this area.

Arab and Jewish Settlement in the Galilee

Israel relates to the Galilee as one of its important development regions. The pre–State settlement history in this area is characterized by a long–established dominant Arab community compared with a quite limited Jewish one. Both peoples were at the time controlled by the British mandatory government which was concerned to avert

98

conflicts of interest between Jews and Arabs. After the establishment of the State in 1948 a new set of relations evolved there between the peoples. The Arab population which lives as a minority in the country, became a demographic and settlement majority in the Central Galilee, with a large natural increase. Following these facts the government initiated a new policy of development with the aim to change the region's demography in favour of Jews.

The Jewish settlement and the demographic achievements in the Galilee till 1948 were not very encouraging. The Arab settlement in this area started much earlier, and continued in succession for hundreds of years, as an extension of Arab settlement that existed in southern Syria and Lebanon. When it spread to northern Palestine the Arab settlement prefered location on the mountains and their flanks, leaving the valleys for agricultural use, and was based mainly on autarchic farms. Its characteristics were location of villages as close as possible to agricultural land, prevention of wasting farm land for building, location of settlements adjacent to the valleys of Sakhnin and Bet Kerem close to the Galilee plain in the west, adjacent to main communications arteries, with exploitation of local water resources, and creation of rural concentrations around Nazareth. The result was that before 1948 there existed in the Galilee 127 Arab villages, with the town of Nazareth as their main urban service center, including about 15,000 inhabitants.

Jewish settlement in the Galilee began only at the end of the 19th century. It started in the Galilee's periphery, mainly in the Upper Hula Valley, around Lake Kinneret, in the southern valleys of Yisreel, Harod and Bet Shean, and along the Western Galilee plain. It formed a sparse U-shape lay-out of kibbutzim and moshavim which surrounded the central Galilean mountainous crest, and which were established in quite inferior geographical conditions regarding water resources, land–use and undrained swamps. A further Jewish penetration into the mountainous Galilee around the turn of the 19th century was also very sparse, with the establishment of settlements as Rosh Pinna, En Zeitim, Yavneel and Ilaniya. It was difficult for Jews to settle in this region because the Arabs refused to sell their land. Till the end of World War 1 there existed in the mountainous part of the Galilee only ten Jewish settlements, and between 1919–1936, only one Jewish settlement, Kefar Ha–Horesh, was added there. The Arab–Jewish disturbances of 1936–1939, and the conclusion of the British Peel Commission to divide the country between Jews and Arabs, set new political goals for the Jewish leadership which emphasized since then the importance of land purchases between the Yisreel Valley in the south and the Lebanese border in the north. The events that took place in the late 1930s led to a new political–territorial view by the Jews who insisted on settlement as a means of maintaining a presence in every possible place, and not just in a regional framework as it was in the past. Because of difficulties in land acquisition by

Jews, only a limited number of settlements was founded in the mountainous area. When the Jewish settlement agencies got more conscious about the importance of executing a territorial policy in the Galilee, a new system of "stockage and tower" settlement was initiated in the middle of the 1930s, which added 21 settlements to the Galilee. But after all these years of efforts made in land acquisition and establishment of settlements, the history of Jewish settlement in the mountainous Galilee did not demonstrate great advantages. Its weight in the demographic balance between Jews and Arabs remained inferior, without many chances to overcome the number of enrooted Arab population which increased during these decades.

Geographical Changes after 1948

After the establishment of the State the reality in the Galilee changed fundamentally. Most of the Arabs who lived in the Galilee for years fled during the 1948–War and left their villages and farms behind. Out of 127 villages, only 50 remained, dispersed all over the region, although some conspicuous concentrations remained around Nazareth, near the Valley of Bet Kerem, and along the Sakhnin – Shefaram axis in the Western Galilee. At that time the Israeli government decided to resettle the Galilee with many Jews, and encouraged for that purpose mainly the new immigrants, who came in those years to Israel in big masses, to settle in the abandoned villages and develop agriculture in the region. At the beginning of the 1950s an intensive settlement process began on Arab vacant lands, and adjacent to them, on the basis of the post 1948–War State land jurisdiction. About 40 new Jewish settlements, mainly moshavim, were established according to this new policy. It was then the first time when a positive demographic balance in favour of the Jews was created in the Galilee. Together with the new development towns of Nazareth–Illit, Shelomi, Hatzor and Qiryat Shemona, and the increase of Jewish population in the existing towns of Zefat, Tiberias and Acre, the rate of Jewish settlers in the Galilee became substantial.

The governmental settlement initiative in the Galilee during the first decade of Israel's existence, has reached impressive results. The Northern District's rate in the total population of Israel reached then 15 per cent, but after a few years later began to decline because of less interest of the immigrants to settle in this area. While in 1961 the rate of Jews in the Northern District was 57.6 per cent, in 1972 it dropped to 54, and in 1992 – to 51 per cent. If we exclude from the Northern District its peripheral valleys, and take into account its central mountainous part only, we may realize, that in 1948 the Jewish population's rate there was 13 per cent, in 1952 it increased enormously to 47.8 by the influx of the new immigrants settlement, but in 1968 dropped to 20 only, and nowadays consolidated on 25 per cent. Land Ownership.

100

The struggle for land in the Galilee between Jews and Arabs has a long record. It evolved for historical reasons, namely because of the inefficient agrarian system that existed in Ottoman regime, the registration and mapping of land administered during the British Mandate regime, and the new land regulations that were formed since the establishment of the State of Israel. During the Ottoman period, out of 15 per cent of land that was then cultivated in the country, only 5 per cent was registered. Unregistered land reverted to the effendis, so that the concentration of land in their possesion became enormous. With the establishment of the State of Israel, a new category of land emerged – land owned by absentees, and by that was meant, land that the Arabs had abandoned in their villages and remained without possesions. This land was transferred to the State and registered as the Trustee of Abandoned Property. On the basis of an Ottoman law, stipulating that land that was not cultivated for three consecutive years reverted to the State, additional land has been acquired by the Israeli authorities. As a result, a constant conflict has developed during the years between the Israeli authorities, who are interested in retaining and concentrating State land as much as possible, and the Arab villagers who wish to enlarge their holdings for either agricultural or constructional purposes. As a result of the long history of struggle for the ownership of land under different regimes, a great rift has developed between State land of various sorts and privately owned land. Jewish jurisdiction on land in the mountainous Galilee extended since the 1950s on 33,500 acres, about 12 per cent of the area, while the Arab jurisdiction extended on about 89,000 acres – 32 per cent of the area, almost three times bigger than that of the Jewish one. On the State land, which comprises 56 per cent of the mountainous Galilee, the Arabs domain about half of the area by actual exploitation in farming and grazing without official ownership. The result was, that the Arabs in the Galilee achieved actually a high priority in land occupation, besides their demographic advantage as a result of high natural increase and of non emigration. Facts as these demonstrate the Jewish weakness in this political territorial struggle between the two peoples in the Galilee.

The intensive development and investment which has been executed in the Galilee after the establishment of the State, mainly during the 1950s and the 1960s, did not attain a Jewish priority in the Central Galilee. The Negev, in the southern part of the country was all the time the most wishful vision of Jewish development, and received priority in investments, settlement and infrastructure. Although the Galilee is geographically much more attractive than the Negev, in climate, in proximity to the central parts of the country, in water resources and in communications, these factors did not influence very much the reality. The new development towns which were built in the Galilee were similar to all the others all over the country, and had no specific attractive features. Most of them did not attract many newcomers, and even lacked with an economic basis and suffered from unemployment. In addition, no consolidated conception has been worked out regarding the physical layout of development towns in the Galilee, should it be linearic, regional, or lateral adjacent to communications routes between west and east, or established adjacent to historical sites. Different conceptions regarding the Jewish settlement system in the Galilee were declared in disorder, and none of them set its seal on the general development process of this region.

It may be concluded, that a long time of weakness that existed in development directives of the Galilee, without any practical approach to its systematic Judaizing, decreased its importance and priority. The Arab sector utilized this situation very well, and increased building, housing, industry and services in its villages, did not emigrate from the region, developed urbanization very intensively, based on capital and income originated from the Jewish sector.

Regional development priority in the 1970s was transfered to the Golan Hights, because of urgent political and security reasons, so that the Galilee remained many years in an inferior situation of development comparatively to other regions in the country.

The Topsites

Israel's response to the demographic situation that had developed in the Central Galilee was a decision to establish new settlement blocs with a large number of topsites in each, with the addition of an industrial zone and a science–based industry in the Galilean town of Karmiel. Each topsite, had to be built on a high mountain from which a large area of landscape could be observed, had to include 100–200 families and to function in an organized form of a community–type settlement with most of its inhabitants working outside in the nearby towns.

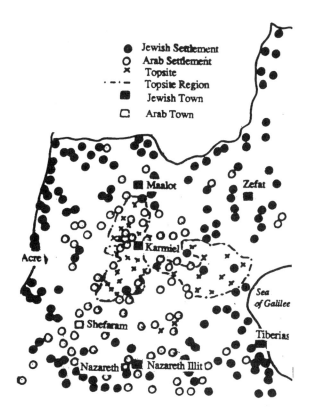

Fig. 20: Jewish and Arab Settlements in the Galilee

Their main function was to prevent Arabs from occupying State land, and acting as buffer zones between Arabn village concentrations. A regional plan which has been prepared in the 1980s envisaged the establishment of 33 topsites in a short span of time. The topsites were established on State land, mostly in rocky areas. Their location has been selected so that from them possible alteration in land–use by the Arabs could be observed. The topsites were established in three blocs: the Tefen bloc in north of the mountainous Galilee, the Segev bloc in the south, and the Tzelafon bloc in the east (Fig. 20).

The implementation of this plan in the 1980s seemed to be exaggerated with its big number of settlements. But within three years many of the planned topsites were established in small enclaves, with short distances between one topsite and the other, and populated mostly by urban inhabitants with a high rate of motorization and commuting possibility. The settlement authorities supported the inhabitants with land allocation and with basic investment in infrastructure.

The results of that plan, after a few years of the topsite's existence in the mountainous Galilee, was as follows: the establishment of the topsites was not theoretically based from the beginning, and that intuition, pressure of time and political circumstances were much more dominant in decision–making than systemathic planning; political intertests played an important role in the erection of topsites in certain sites which were not always successful; no occupation planning existed, so that the settlers did not have any local economic basis for their existence; although there was some success in the fact that population was dispersed all over the mountainous area of the Central Galilee, the number of a few thousand of settlers that live there today did not justify the enormous investments which were made, while their increase in population is still slow; only two thirds of the topsites succeeded economically, while all the rest failed. Anyhow, the establishment of topsites in the Galilee might be evaluated as an Israeli success in the dispersion of Jewish population in a difficult terrain of the Galilee in a few years, and in dominating governmental lands which were in the past unsettled.

Future Prospects in the Galilee

The Judaizinq of the Galilee aimed to attain, as said, a Jewish majority and a settlement distribution with a dominate Jewish presence. The goal was to achieve accelerated growth of population which will stop the demographic decrease of Jews in the area. Quantitatively it may be achieved by encouraging urban growth of cities, but then the spatial effect will be weakened, and if scattering the population in agricultural settlements on the mountainous area, the quantitative effect will be reduced. A solid economic base for development is also very difficult to achieve in the Galilee because its lacks in natural economic resources and opportunities for private initiative development.

Regarding the future of the Galilee, it may be said, that the unsystematic development of both rural and urban settlement, the inferior dominance of State land, the negative Jewish demographic balance, the declining attraction of development towns and the absense of integration on the regional level are deficiencies which have to be improved. No much hope should be given to the topsites as a means of Judaizing of the Galilee. An overall regional improvement can be achieved if the development bodies in Israel will view the Galilee as a region of vital importance and will be prepared to invest in it most of their available resources.

The Challenge of the Negev

One of the lofty aims of Jewish colonization in the Land of Israel was to settle the arid Negev. But the sequence of settlement activities since World War 2 indicates that although modern means were available for establishing new forms of rural and urban settlements, no significant breakthrough occurred in the zone of aridity along the Beer Sheba valley. The town of Arad in the east and the townlets of Dimona and Yeruham in the south–east are the remotest development sites in that region. Further initiatives to skip over the entire zone, by establishing rural settlements in the mountainous area of the Central Negev or increasing the population of the townlet Mitzpe Ramon, did not lead to encouraging results.

It seems, that Israel's governmental bodies have accepted, consciously or subconsciously, the fact that the northern Negev should be the southern settlement frontier of the country, with the exception of the Elat region along the Gulf in the south, behind which a backyard may be created for noxious industries and polluting installations, for which no reasonable place can be found in the north. The concentration of sedentarized Bedouins east of Beer Sheva, the location of chemical industries at Ramat Hovav, the nuclear reactor at Dimona, military open ranges in the central Negev, new ammunition factories to be established at Ramat Beqa, and the planned site of solid disposal on the sands of Halutza in the western Negev, are only a few examples of a new kind of backyard–frontier which is developing. Lack of space in Central and Northern Israel, the urgent need to supply jobs for thousands of immigrants, and the inability to expand the southern frontier by traditional means, have now created an unexpected and unplanned desert fringe area with special dynamics of expansion.

Despite the expressed ideology of the government to reclaim and settle the desert, the gap between the affluent core and the relatively impoverished Negev periphery is growing. The Negev, Israel's vast arid desert region, has less than seven percent of the country's population, but occupies nearly two–thirds of the country's land mass. Once considered essential for Israel's development, the region now suffers from neglect. Apart from the 1950s, little effort has been made to develop the region. The Negev's economic, social, cultural and educational infrastructure can however be improved through a regional approach to development. Lately has the government formulated a proposal for a new national plan for eight million inhabitants in Israel around the year 2020. This proposal is being presented to the National Board for consideration and to the government for approval, and is intended to replace the plan adopted in 1985. A principle aim of the population distribution plans, as the new 2020 plan, has always been to encourage the growth and development of the Negev as against the metropolitan area and the central coastal plain. It is believed by the planners, that the strenghtening of frontier areas as the Negev can best be achieved in a national context when the necessary efforts and funds are appropriated from the total resources of the nation. In the past, Israel made some significant progress in the development of the Negev. In 1948, the Negev numbered only 14,200 inhabitants, and in 1994 – approximately 380,000, which means, that seven percent of the total population of the country in 1994 resided in the Negev, as oposed to 0.2 percent in 1948.

Development of Tourism in the Frontier

The Negev is still a frontier land, in the sense that it is little developed, but a development boom is due in the near future. In contrast to the heavy and pollutinq industries to be transfered from northern Israel to the Negev, tourism development could be a much better proposal for this region, based on the well–known interest of the public and the hunger for cultural tourism and recreation in the nature. Such an approach may include preparing of an inventory of the prominent geological, ecological, archeological and cultural assets of oustanding interest and quality of preservation; the assemblage of educational tools that will present the assets to the public in a most attractive mode and in a tourist and recreational environment; and preparing a conceptual program for the development of a tourism network that will expose travellers to a maximum diversity of the different landscapes.

Up until a few years ago, the Negev had an uncoordinated selection of tourist attractions developed on a local scale, mainly run by each municipality. In recent years, it was suggested that a regional authority should be set up to handle the problems of developing the region by the potential of tourism. Priorities include encouraging economic investments in a wide variety of projects, as well as setting up the basic tourist infrastructure. Such projects may provide much needed employment opportunities to a region with a high rate of unemployment. The Negev is still one of

Israel's less developed regions, an area of outstanding natural beauty and, in spite of its harsh climate, it provides opportunities for long–term tourist projects. Selecting suitable projects, financing their infrastructure and maintenance, marketing, and the training of personell, are all continuing objectives (Fig. 21).

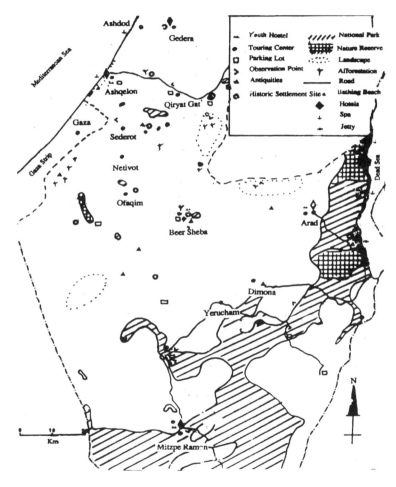

Fig. 21: Touristic Sites in the Northern Negev

One of the promising future projects for tourism development is the Gulf of Aqaba. This Gulf is a beautiful and rare ecosystem whose waters do not recognize political boundaries. Sustainable development of this frontier region is essential for all of the Gulf bordering states: Egypt, Israel, Jordan and Saudi Arabia. The Gulf of Aqaba is Jordan's only outlet to the sea and also serves as an important port for Israel. The Gulf is threatened by unregular coastal development, oil spills, municipal sewage and unregulated tourist activity and litter. The short distance seperating the port cities Aqaba and Elat highlights the need for cooperation of the Gulf and its surroundings to be safeguarded. In the long run, effective regional environmental protection depends upon each state's ability to administer environmental policy. Recognizing that regional coordination is necessary in order to protect the Gulf, the coastal states have shown lately a trend of cooperation. The political obstacles which existed in the past may be removed by the nowadays peace negotiations between the countries, which is important to plan the future of the area.

A joint development project between the Gulf countries may yield many benefits. The unique climate and natural environment of the Elat–Aqaba region provides a significant tourist attraction. However certain conditions must be present in order to encourage tourism such as political stability, secure mobility and appropriate services. The countries controlling the Gulf might accept the idea of a free tourism zone and turning the coast into a single region in which goods, services and tourists can move freely. Planning for free tourism also requires coordination of trade, relations and taxation. It also requires cooperation and coordination between the municipal authorities in the region as in infrastructure services, transportation and international communications, coordinated environmental policy, law and order, and regional planning. Such an approach might lead to a significant increase in the number of hotels and guest rooms, an increase in the number of tourists, creation of employment and jobs for residents in the surrounding areas, significant increase in the region's population, and in the stabilizing the peace in the entire Middle East.

As a central component in its geographical sequence, the Negev's potential role in the tourist industry is to increase in the event of peace. The potential for tourism in the Negev, in a situation of peace, may be the best solution for the Negev. A state of peace and the reduced fear and tension resulting from it, will affect the tourism sector more than any other sector in the country. For thousands of years the Negev has served as a link between East and the West. This link left its mark on roads and on sequence of sites in the region. Its discontinuity, brought about by the closing of internationl borders, caused the region to loose some of its characteristic natural, archeological and historic uniquness. Once this continuity is reestablished, and a new sequence is opened, the attraction of the sites and routes will be increased. Mutual cooperation might serve as a foundation for far-reaching projects with advantages such as size and positive external influence.

Geography and Policy of the New Development Towns

More than thirty new towns, in which about 18% of its Jewish population live today, have been established in Israel between 1948 and 1963. It was the most important and outstanding phenomenon in changing the settlement map of a new–born state. This chapter analyzes the ideas, aims and ways of their establishment, the policy which stands behind them, and their degree of function in the absorption process of the mass–immigration at the beginning in the 1990s (Efrat, 1994a).

Reasons for the Establishment of New Towns

It is difficult to say whether the government of Israel had made the decision to create new towns at the time of the establishment of the tate in 1948. The decision to build new towns was forced upon the settlement agencies mainly because of the pressure of immigration from European, Asian and African countries after the World War 2 and the absorption needs. Not all the immigrants arriving between 1948 and 1953 could then be absorbed into the agricultural sector due to land and water limitations. It was felt that other solutions should be found, and that something should be done in the urban sector. The establishment of new towns for the purpose of immigrant absorption and the distribution of the population appeared to be a reasonable solution for the problem. Once this route for immigration absorption was chosen, the settlement bodies did not forget their traditional agricultural ideology of the past. So in the planning of the urban settlements there was an intermingling of ideas resulting in new towns of low density with one storey houses and yards for agricultural purposes. This penetration of agricultural concepts in the planning of the new towns greatly influenced their shape from the beginning. The new towns did not immediately become urban ideological goals. For at lest 10–15 years this semi–urban approach continued, and no social or urban ideology developed regarding urbanization (Efrat, 1989).

The Town's Hierarchy

The Israeli planners of the 1950s did not develop original urban concepts of their own because of their lack of experience. Rather, they attempted to apply planning models that were widely accepted in other countries. One well–liked model of urban spatial distribution was the hierarchy pattern based on the establishment of agricultural settlements which had a direct relationship with small or medium–sized urban centers, and these were in contact with larger centers, townlets or towns, and these had connections to a primate town which was at the top of the settlement pyramid. The fundamental approach to the new towns was not very revolutionary, rather it was very conservative and was taken from European systems (Dash et al., 1964).

Due to fifty years of extensive pioneering in Israel, from the beginning of the century till the establishment of the State, there were many agricultural settlements, such as kibbutzim (communal settlements) and moshavim (smallholders' settlements). No recognizable development was found in the middle stage of the hierarchy model, so that the establishment of medium–sized towns in Israel became the intermediary between the large towns and the small agricultural settlements. The first purpose was to complete the missing links in the former settlement layout via the establishment of medium–sized development towns which would be used as service centers by their agricultural surroundings.

The new settlement hierarchy was built in five levels, beginning with the village at the lowest level, until the large town at the top, in order to change the nodality which had enrooted itself during the urban system of the past. This hierarchy presented the following types of settlements:

Type A – villages with 500 inhabitants

Type B - village centers with 2,000 inhabitants each

Type C – semi–urban centers with 6,000–12,000 inhabitants each

Type D – medium–sized towns with 40,000–60,000 inhabitants

Type E – large towns with 100,000 inhabitants or more

The village center was to supply services to 3–5 villages around it. The semi–urban center was to provide services to 30 villages in a radius of 10 kilometers, and the services located there would be of a higher rank. The medium–sized towns were to have a concentration of governmental institutions, banks, hospitals and factories. The large town was to be given the status of a regional capital and was to maintain connections with other large towns in the country. The planners made great efforts to establish settlements of types B, C, and D because of their potential to absorb new immigrants.

Within a few years these centers became the weak and problematic links in the entire national urban network. The concept was to create a new urban center under the condition that it would not be disconnected from agriculture. The population of such a center had to be small in size and located in agricultural surroundings. These centers were later critisized as being too small to develop an urban lifestyle in them. Perhaps the local reason behind the construction of small centers was that the planners had to change

110

gradually their settlement ideology and to transfer it to the type of town planning forced upon them by the existing realities.

The new towns and the different semi–urban centers had to be integrated into veteran regions with established and economical bases. The regions where the new towns were located had been settled for many years by the kibbutzim and moshavim. These new towns could only supply low–level services to the veteran settlements which from the first beginning were not sympathetic nor attracted to these centers.

The absence of an interrelationship between the immigrant towns and the veteran settlements prevented additional attempts to establish new towns on one hand, while also discouraging the improvement of services in the already existing towns, so that most of them developed slowly without impetus, and with the great concern of solving the daily problems of their own inhabitants on other hand.

Geographical Distribution of Development towns

The location of the development towns was decided to very according criteria, the directed functions the towns would have along with suitable geographical conditions. From a geographical perspective the distribution of development towns was not particularly appropriate. Many were located too close together as Ofaqim, Sederot and Netivot in the Western Negev, while others were situated near large towns. In areas like the Eastern Galilee or the Arava in the south, no development towns were established. Town location was the result of practical and political reasons, immediate needs and because of inexpensive land (Fig.22).

Upon classifying the new towns according to year and place of establishment we find that since statehood, about forty new settlements were founded and populated. Of those 36 were given the status of a local authority or town. Town distribution according to founding date shows significant variations in the number established during each time period. The maximum number of towns was founded between 1949–1950. Although ten were established in two years, it should be mentioned, that most of these towns previously existed and had been abandoned by the Arabs during the War of Independence (1948–1949). Because they were already there, immigrants were directed to them and shortly occupied all the abandoned structure.

Since 1951 onwards new housing has been established. The time period between 1948 and 1956 was when the majority of 24 new urban Jewish settlements were added to the map of Israel. Since 1957 new town establishment has ceased and most of the work in them was concentrated in improving their overall inner structure. This retention came with a decrease in the number of immigrants, and those who came later were directed to live in existing towns. In the 1960s two additional towns were founded, Arad

111

in 1961 and Karmiel in 1964 (Efrat, 1974). They were different from previously established towns because their populations were selected from people living in Israel for many years and immigrants, and from the beginning the towns' construction was modern. Since 1964 no new town has been added in the country within its 'Green Line' borders, except the town of Modiin, east of the Tel Aviv periphery, which is now under construction.

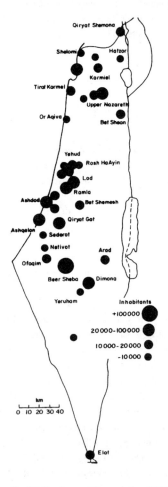

Fig. 22: Development Towns in Israel 1995

The new towns classification according to regions in the country shows that until 1950 the central district was the main location of the new towns and to a lesser extend, the northern district. Because absorption initially took place in abandoned towns which were located in the coastal plain the main population increase took place there also. For towns being created without the basis of a former infrastructure, priority was given to the southern district where most of the towns were built between 1951–1956. It is apparent that the first new towns outside of the central district were located in the northern part of the country, where veteran Jewish populations were settled, and where there was a political need to overcome the Arab population. An additional classification of towns according to their infrastructure shows that out of 36, 24 were completely new, four were mixed between old and new, and eight were built on abandoned Arab infrastructure.

The influence of geography on the distribution of the new towns was minimal. With the exception of location like the Gulf of Elat, the transit area between the higher lowland and the 'Corridor of Jerusalem', and even the upper Hula Valley where new towns were objectively needed, town location was a matter of choice. Towns were not established on the basis of local natural resources and because the distance from one place to another within the country was so minimal with the exception of the southern Negev, it was not imperative to develop too many towns. Since water and energy sources were extremely limited, they were not taken into account in locating towns. Location, therefore, was primarily the result of the following factors: policy, topography, climate and land ownership. Establishing towns in the Negev was easily facilitated as almost all the land there was owned by the state.

The New Towns' Regional Impact

Since 92% of Israel's territory is in the hands of the Land Administration, the decision to establish development towns was not difficult to make. Most of the immigrant housing was constructed in peripheral developmemt regions, thus contributing to population dispersal in towns in Israel. From the perspective of time, towns were established with the waves of immigration, as well as geographical locations, because initially they were constructed in the country's center and then shifted to the north and later reached the south. The Negev was opened for urban settlement only in the 1950s, after roads had been paved and new projects constructed. Once begun, development increased at an accelerated rate from year to year, so that the southern district contained 13% of the country's population. The weight of the southern district expanded, so that almost half of the immigrants were concentrated there. The advantage of the Negev had over the more populated areas was, that the growth of agriculture and

113

urbanization there occurred simultaneously and in conjunction with each other. In the north, for instance, a veteran agricultural structure existed which operated much more efficiently than the new towns. This was not the case in the south where agricultural settlement was based on new moshavim which needed a strong relationship with the new towns, thus bringing about an increase in urbanization. The new towns promoted the populating of peripheral regions of the country, in the northern district by 67% and in the southern district by 83%. Between the middle of the 1960s till the end of the 1980s, the growth of new towns decreased due to lower immigration rates, but increased again with the Russian–Jewish mass–immigration which started in 1990 and continued in the 1990s. The new towns have always responded to immigration ebb and flow.

The composition of the population in the new towns was not planned in advance but it was well known that it would be primarily made up of new immigrants and not by veteran inhabitants of the country. It was difficult to predict the immigration flow and thus the population rate of the towns. It should be recalled, that the immigration was a very strong phenomenon which the country was unprepared to handle. In 1948 more than 100,000 immigrants arrived. In 1949 – twice that amount came to Israel. In the past, most of the immigrants were young, single, socially and economically ambitious people or pioneers with Zionist mentality. The immigrants of the 1950s came with large families and with a high percentage of children and elderly. While prior to 1948 most of the immigrants came from Europe, from 1948 to mid 1950s only 5.5% came from that continent while the majority came from Asian and African countries.

Although not all of the immigrants were directed to development towns they did influence their size and character. In the new towns which were established until 1951, 120,000 people lived. Between 1952–1954, four new towns were added which were inhabited by 22,000 people. Between 1958–1960 a decrease in the population of developmemt towns began. Most of the new towns expanded on their own as a result of natural increase and internal immigration expressed by the construction of additional housing.

In the last years a greater interest in the structure and quality of life of the new towns has arisen. A new wave of rehabilitation has appeared in many of them. Even the construction style was greatly improved. More compact and higher housing was built, their central business districts were improved, institutions were constructed, industrial projects were promoted reestablishing an employment base and even private enterprise was permitted.

Conclusions

It may be concluded that the urban layout in Israel was too rapid, while during one decade only, most of the new urban facts were created. Beside the gradual growth of the veteran towns, a new wave of towns appeared and gained priorities in investments, in housing projects and in populating, and assigned new goals for inner–migration, and a new geography of settlement distribution. The urban layout has never been planned to the end. But because a geographical distribution of towns is a very rigid system, it is almost impossible to change it, so the only way that remains is to improve permanently the infrastructure of these development towns with the hope that in the future they will be well integrated in the Israel's urban system.

With the new mass–immigration of the Russian–Jews in 1989 1995, and the Ethiopian immigration with more than 50,000 people in a short time, the government believed to improve its unsuccessful experiences of previous years and to encourage again a distribution of population according to obsolete concepts. But the current immigration is basicly different in its cultural, economic and social background, and is not reacting in accordance with these concepts. The new immigrants do not intend to go to all places where the government wants them to go, while many of the development towns are not attractive enough for them, more to the Ethiopians but less for the Russians, mainly because of lack of occupation possibilities and level of services, a fact which stresses basic failures in the scope of the development towns that were established in Israel during the 1950s.

Israel's Strategy of Handling the Russia–Jewish Immigration

At the end of 1988 the Soviet Union has opened the gates, and a long struggle to "Let My People Go" has almost seemed to come to an end. While the exodus of the Russian Jews had almost one destination to Israel, the State was facing since then one of the most difficult absorption challenges it has ever had. Hundreds of thousands of Russian Jews have arrived to Israel since then and it is expected that hundreds of thousands may be arriving till the end of the century. It is supposed that in a small country as Israel, with its own 4.3 million Jewish inhabitants, these masses of immigration will provide a momentum to an overall change in the country's pattern of settlement and even a modification in its basic pattern of population dispersal.

The main characteristics of the current Russian–Jewish immigration to Israel are the big masses which arrived in a short time, the ability of the newcomers to choose their places of living by their own, because of a new absorption system that has been introduced by governmental authorities, and the heavy economic burden under which

Israel's government tried to provide the immigrants with accomodation and employment.

This new situation in Israel arose a few geographical problems which will be discussed below: What is the current pattern of the Russian–Jewish immigrants distribution over the country comparatively to the past? Which are the regions and towns mostly prefered by the immigrants? To what an extent do the immigrants bring to a change in the existing trends of population distribution? And how do the governmental housing projects, which are now under construction, fit with the places where they want to live?

Characteristics of the Russian–Jewish Immigration to Israel

Since the establishment of the State in 1948 till 1983 the number of Soviet–Jewish immigrants reached 180,139 which comprised not more than 10% of the total number of immigrants who came to Israel (Central Bureau of Statistics, 1988). During most of the years the annual immigration rates from the Soviet Union were not so high. High immigration rates occurred in 1957 after the Sinai War, between 1971–1974, and during the years 1978–1979. The immigraton rates dropped again during the 1980s till the end of that decade when a mass–immigration took place again.

Since the end of 1988 the whole situation has totally changed. In 1989 about 13,000 Russian Jews arrived, while in 1990 the number increased to a peak of about 189,000(!). It meant that in one year the Jewish immigration from Russia was more than the total immigration since the establishment of the State of Israel. During the first half of 1991 another 50,000 Russian–Jewish immigrants have arrived, and since then about 60,000–70,000 Russian Jewish immigrants arrived to Israel annually.

There was also an increase in the rate of the Russian–Jews relatively to the total numbers of immigrants. While in 1988 they comprised only 16.5 percent, in 1989 their rate increased to 52 percent, in 1990 – to 86.6 percent, and in 1991 – to more than 90 percent. It means that what is happening now in Israel is a rapid outstanding demographic phenomenon with geographical and economic consequenses in location of population, housing, in creating jobs, in establishing services, in building new neighborhoods, and eventually in changing the settlement map of Israel.

The Direct Absorption

The demographic and economic composition of the Russian Jewish immigrants of the 1990s is very similar to that of the 1970s. Their cultural and economic background is the same, they belong to an urban population with liberal professions and are generally high–educated. Most of them arrived to Israel with no ideological or zionistic

116

motives, but mainly because of the strong awakenings of antisemitism which appear now in Russia, their fear of pogroms and the spirit of 'GlasMost' which lightened their immigration. It could be that a part of them does not even see Israel as their final destination, but as a life–boat before trying to immigrate to somewhere else.

The new system of Russian–Jewish immigrants support which has been introduced by the Israeli government in this case was, that the governmental and public bodies were not involved in the immigrants' free choice for living, but gave them a lump sum of money per family for all their needs in the first year of absorption. Such a policy was very different from that of the beginnig of the 1950s, when the Israeli government, in order to absorb a mass–immigration from Asian and African countries, established absorption centers and distributed them all over the country, where immigrants received dwelling for a few months and facilities for learning Hebrew. At the same time three types of temporary sites were established: transit camps, labour villages and small semi–urban centers, where the immigrants could settle till their next step of habitation. In spite of their temporariness they enabled to settle many of them to the Galilee in the north, to the Negev in the south and to the mountainous Corridor of Jerusalem, and later on – to the 30 development towns which were established in the 1950s. It was then a reasonable way to implement the official plans for population dispersal, to populate unsettled regions and fringe areas along the borderlines and to strenghten Israel's sovereignty on its territory. The poorer and the less professional the immigrants were, the easier was to direct them to unsettled areas on a basis of agricultural and non professional employment.

That was not the present case with the Russian–Jewish immigrants who came with an urban background, lived and worked in European towns, were high–professional educated and were therefore seeking for dwelling and occupation in urban, veteran and well–developed settlements. While the majority of them continue to opt for direct absorption in the different parts of the country, it provides a good opportunity to follow their priorities and preferences for settlement and dwelling which is, undoubtly, determined by the inventory of flats, rent prices on a free market and sources of employment. The fact that the potential of available dwelling is higher in the northern and southern regions of the country, with less employment opportunities, while a smaller potential of dwelling with high prices but with better chances to find a job, exists in the central regions, was a test–case for Israel's population distribution policy (Efrat, 1990). The fact that more than 90% of the current immigrants opted direct absorption, may be a threat to the governmental policy of population distribution.

Spatial Distribution of the Russian–Jews

The settlement pattern of the 180,139 Soviet–Jews who came to Israel between 1948–1983 indicates that 20,790 settled in Tel Aviv, 13,395 – in Jerusalem and 12,632 – in Haifa (Central Bureau of Statistics, 1988). It means that in the three big cities 46,817 or 25.6 percent of all the Soviet Jews were concentrated after 35 years of habitation in Israel (Fig. 23). Other concentrations of Soviet–Jews, between 5,000–10,000 each, have developed in smaller towns as: Qiryat Yam, Netanya, Ramat Gan, Holon, Bat Yam, Rishon Le Ziyyon, Ashdod and Beer Sheba, many of them situated in the coastal plain and a few of them even in the Tel Aviv conurbation. 15 smaller

Fig. 23: Distribution of Soviet-Jews in Israel 1948 - 1983

concentrations of 2,000–5,000 each, and 21 others with less than 2,000 each, were also to be found along the coastal plain. Only a few concentrations of Soviet–Jews existed on the central mountainous axis of the country, along the eastern Karmiel – Upper Nazareth – Afula axis and along the more remote axis of Zefat- Bet Shean-Arad–Dimona. It should be mentioned that only 10 percent of the Soviet–Jews went to the development towns which were established in the 1950s.

The main conclusions regarding the spatial distribution of the Russian–Jews in 1983, who immigrated to Israel since the establishment of the State (1948), and who might be a lodestone for the newcomers are, that they are in principle an urban population with an urban mentality which seeks the big cities and the veteran places along the coastal plain for living, where the chances for employment are better. They did not go to peripheral areas, and not even to development towns where a majority of Jewish Asian and African immigrants reside. They also did not refer to the administered areas in Judea, Samaria and the Gaza Strip or to the annexed area of the Golan Heights.

Spatial Distribution of Russian–Jewish Immigrants under Direct Absorption

If we examine the spatial distribution of the Russian Jewish immigrants during the year 1989 who opted the direct absorption program we may indicate, that 10,657 out of 12,842 whose addresses were registered, prefered the towns of Haifa and Netanya where groups of more than 1,000 each were found (Ministry of Absorption, 1990). Groups of 500–1,000 appeared in Qiryat Yam, Tel Aviv, Bat Yam, Holon, Rishon Le Ziyyon, Rehovot and Jerusalem, while in all the other 36 places the groups of Russian immigrants were smaller. In the Galilee and in the Judean Mountains the groups included less than 200 each. None of them have settled south to Beer Sheba, and only 1,403 (13.1 percent) of them went to development towns.

But how has this trend changed in 1990? During that year a mass–immigration of 184,198 Russian–Jews occurred, the biggest one Israel ever had, which brought to the country more Russian–Jews than forty years before (Ministry of Absorption, 1991). In that year big concentrations of Russian immigrants, who opted the direct absorption program, were to be found in the four towns of Tel Aviv, Haifa, Jerusalem and Netanya with more than 10,000 immigrants in each. Seven other concentrations of 5,000–10,000 were along the coastal plain and one in Beer Sheba, and 20 more concentrations of 1,000 5,000 each, with 15 of them in the coastal plain (Fig. 24). The dispersion of this mass–immigration reached Zefat, Karmiel and Upper Nazareth in the north and Ashqelon and Arad in the south. To the development towns refered 24,435 immigrants (12.7 percent). The trend of this wave of immigration was the doubling or trippling of the existing concentration of 1989. Beside the coastal plain only Jerusalem and Beer

Sheba were relatively attractive. The distribution of the Russian–Jewish immigrants during 1991 1994 showed almost the same trend of concentration along the coastal plain, with a slight move towards the south and the north.

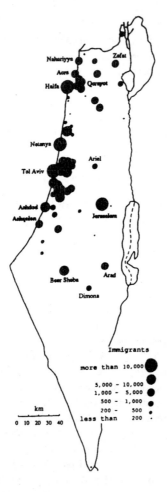

Fig. 24: Distribution of Russian-Jewish Immigrants 1990

The main conclusions which could be drawn from the direct absorption were, that the immigrants were not eager to settle in fringe areas because of security problems, they had no pioneering motivations, they were not interested in Judea and Samaria and, to a certain extent, even not in development towns. They highly prefered the central parts of the country and the big veteran cities. Till now they have not changed the basic pattern of the settlement priorities of their predessors, with some few exceptions.

If we examine the distribution of the Russian–Jewish immigrants during the years 1988–1994 in the four main regions of the country: the Galilee and Haifa area, Tel Aviv area and the central coastal plain, Jerusalem area and the Negev in the south, we may find that about a third of the immigrants went to the Galilee, about 9 percent Jerusalem area, more than a half went to Tel Aviv and its surroundings, and only a small part of the immigrants went to the Negev in the south.

The main trends which could be observed in the regional division are, therefore, population increase of the coastal plain, a decrease in Jerusalem area because of a lack in dwelling and the security problems, a gradual increase in the northern region because of a few relatively attractive development towns as Karmiel and Upper Nazareth, and a small proportion of immigrants in the Negev because of its remoteness from the coastal plain and its semi–arid climate(Fig. 25)

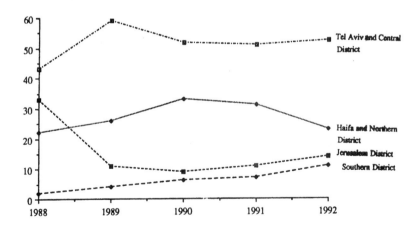

Fig. 25: Russian-Jewish Immigrants according to Regions

If we compare the proportion of the Russian–Jewish immigrants in these four regions to the proportion of the veteran Jewish population who lives there, we may find, that 51 percent of the immigrants settled in the Tel Aviv area as against 44 percent of the veteran population, 9.7 percent of the immigrants settled in the Jerusalem area as against 12.2 percent, 6.3 percent in the Negev as against 12 percent, while in the north – the proportion remained almost equal, 30 percent as against 32 percent.

In a research on the absorption potential of the new immigrants in rural settlements, based on a sample survey of 630 new immigrants, who lived and studied in 'Hebrew learning' schools, it was found that the main factor in choosing place for living was occupation possibilities, while the second factor was distance from borderlines because of security danger (Finkel and Margulies, 1991). The first place of settling had a decisive weight in the immigrants' choice but was determined by the absorption abilities of the place in providing them reasonable facilities. Any supply of dwelling, but without job opportunities, will give no chance for their willingness to stay at their place. More than 50 percent expressed their wish to live in the central coastal plain, 25 percent – in the north, the same percentage in the south, and 10 percent – in Jerusalem area. Only 5 percent were ready to stay in rural areas. The tendency of living in urban areas was found, therefore, to be very dominant among them.

Governmental Plans for the Russian–Jewish Absorption

Two governmental authorities in Israel were involved in preparing plans for the absorption of the Russin–Jewish mass immigration, the Ministry of the Interior and the Ministry of Building and Housing. With the arrival of the Russian–Jews the government ordered the Ministry of the Interior on 19 June 1990 to prepare an outline scheme for the absorption of the expected immigrants with the aim "to offer a policy and to consolidate a framework for their absorption on the basis of existing and proposed physical, social, environmental and economic plans". It meant actually, to adjust a former plan of population distribution to the present new situation. The directive was to absorb a million of immigrants in the next five years and by that to strenghten Jerusalem, the Galilee and the Negev. The former plan which was approved by the government in 1985, with a target of five million inhabitants in Israel in the year 1992, was not found to be realistic. In many towns and settlements the planned population targets were not achieved. No meaningful Jewish population increase occurred in the Galilee, nor in the Negev, and no planned decrease happened in the population of the coastal plain.

A new plan was therefore prepared by the Ministry of the Interior for a target of seven million inhabitants towards the year 2010. According to this plan the northern district should double its populatioin during the next years, the southern district should reach a million inhabitants, and the Tel Aviv district should grow only by 250,000 inhabitants (23%). The central district was supposed to grow less than the northern and the southern ones, and also the Haifa district. The increase in the population of Judea and Samaria should be up to 250,000, and the big part of this increment should come from the new immigrants.

It seems that this plan was mostly a wishful dream and not very realistic either because its Achilles' heel is the lack of employment sources which are very difficult to create for so many people in all these places. Those who will be refered to peripheral areas may find there very poor infrastructure and services which are not even sufficient for the veteran population. Till this plan was approved and implemented most of the newcomers found by themselves the better places to reside and created new spatial facts which were quite opposite to this plan.

Fig. 26: Governmental Plan for the Distribution of Russian-Jewish Immigrants

Another plan which has been prepared by the Ministry of Building and Housing was designed for 200,000 new immigrants till 1994. In order to reach this target the plan proposed to settle more than 25,000 immigrants in the new town of Modiin and in the development town of Bet Shemesh (Fig. 26).

Six other towns were supposed to absorb 8,000–15,000 immigrants each: Jerusalem, Beer Sheba, Ashdod, Karmiel, Maalot, and the new site of Zafit. Concentrations of 3,000–7,000 were planned for Zefat, Upper Nazareth and for the new site of Givat Shaal in the Upper Galilee, for Netanya and Ashqelon, and for the two development towns Sederot and Ofaqim in the northern Negev. What was very striking in this plan was the fact that the prefered areas by the Ministry of Building and Housing for establishing housing projects for the immigrants were the northern and eastern Galilee, the eastern coastal plain along the former 'Green Line', which once existed as a borderline between Israel and Samaria, and the northern and north eastern Negev. It should be stressed that most of these sites were never prefered by the Russian–Jewish immigrants.

In this plan the towns and places which were prefered by the immigrants were missing. No priority was given to Tel Aviv, Netanya, Ramat Gan, Rishon Le Ziyyon, Holon and Bat Yam, for instance. It seems that the government aimed to settle the immigrants according to its national guidelines for distribution of population although no real facilities and basic employment sources exist till now in most of these places. But ironically, the plan received a serious treatment by the government.

The conflict between the free choice of the immigrants' settlement against the governmental spatial directions for distribution of population appears now as a battle–field between two forces which may influence Israel's urban settlement pattern in the future.

Conclusions and Consequences

The only experience in absorption of mass–immigration in Israel occurred in the 1950s, when hundreds of thousands Jews from Asian and African countries arrived and were dispersed in peripheral areas on an agricultural economic basis in immigrant villages and in new development towns which were established for them. While many of the peripheral areas were unpopulated and most of the immigrants were non–professional and came without financial means, it was quite easy to locate them wherever the government was interested to. During the years these immigrants tried to improve their living in these villages and in the new development towns. Their settlements created a rim in the northern and eastern Galilee, along the eastern coastal plain, in the 'Jerusalem Corridor' and in the northern Negev, wheras the veteran population, which lived on an established economic position, remained in the big cities and in other urban settlements.

These immigrants tried from time to time to come closer to the centers of economic and cultural activities of the country, but without much success. The distribution plans of the 1950s succeeded only partially, and the fact is that only 18 percent of the total Jewish population lives in these places. The allotment of budgets for infrastructure and services in the new settlements were never sufficient, so that the economic and social growth potential of the periphery as a whole, to absorb more people, became weaker and almost impossible.

With the new mass–immigration of the Russian–Jews since 1990 the government tried to improve its unsuccessful experience of previous years and to enforce again a distribution of population according to obsolete concepts. But as mentioned, the current immigration is basicly different in its cultural, economic and social background, and may not react in accordance with these concepts. In order to absorb them in a reasonable and promising way they should not be enforced to go to peripheral areas. They ought to be absorbed on an economic basis and employment sources which exist and could be enlarged in the central parts of the country. If the distribution of the Russian–Jewish population is nevertheless needed, it should not be remoter than the outer rim of the central coastal plain.

A delicate situation has been created in Israel. On one hand the government is interested to increase Jewish population in Israel, and has even prepared a plan for a more million Jews to come in a decade. The present mass immigration shortened suddenly this period into 3–4 years and enforced the government to change its plans and to build thousands of new houses wherever land was available and to create new jobs in all the sections for thousands of newcomers, a mission impossible to be executed in a short time.

On other hand, the new immigrants did not intend to go to all the places where the government wanted them to go, and the direct absorption program enabled them to choose, to some degree, the places where they prefered to live. The government is now in a hurry to build new houses and to create new jobs under economic and social pressures of the immigrants.

It is believed that if the government will not find the appropriate solutions for dwelling and employment in due time, the Russian–Jews will begin to emigrate again, and those who are still waiting in Russia may retreat from their willingness to come to Israel. In that case Israel may loose of a great historic chance to absorb an enormous mass educated high–professional Jews.

The conflict is, as seen, territorial and economic, and very effective in that short span of time. Even if the government will succeed in absorbing most of these immigrants it would change the whole concept of the distribution of population in Israel which existed till now and may definitelv chanqe the geographical settlement map of the country.

The Minorities of Israel in their Political Circumstances

The State of Israel, which has made great efforts in the absorption of hundreds of thousand Jewish immigrants during the 1950s and the 1960s, has prepared for them a physical, economic and social infrastructure in the country, and has integrated them into the veteran population's life, has unfortunately not done enough for the Arab minorities. The Arabs who live in the sovereign territory of Israel form a relative big share of the country's population, they own much land in regions where they reside, and are very much involved in Israel's politics. The minorities which live as in "a state within a state", deserve a more serious treatment from the Israel governmental bodies, because of their demographic weight in the total population and their occupance of large areas along the Israeli borderlines with Judea and Samaria.

Demographic Background

The following demographic and geographical data may illustrate the minorities' situation in Israel. At the end of 1991 they totaled 914,200 inhabitants – about 18 per cent of the population in Israel. Their share in the total population was higher than that of the Jewish one which resides in the new development towns. Most of the minorities are concentrated in the Northern District, including the Upper and Lower Galilee. Out of about 914,200 inhabitants who lived in this district in 1991, 48 percent were minorities, as against 52 percent Jews, a fact which demonstrates, that both peoples in the Galilee are demographically in almost balance. In the central mountainous part of the Galilee, excluding the valleys of Hula and Lake Kinneret in the east, the Valley of Yisreel in the south, and the coastal plain of Acre, which performed since the late 1880s as the cradle of Jewish settlement in the northern part of the Land of Israel, the minorities comprise about 75 percent of the total population. The rate of the minorities in the Northern District is 2.8 times bigger than it comprises in the total population of Israel, which reaches 16.9 percent only. The number of the minorities' settlements in the Northern District was in 1991 – 83, and they comprised a quarter of all the settlements in this region. The number of their settlements with more than 5,000 inhabitants were 26, among them was the town of Nazareth with its 50,000 inhabitants, and Shefaram – with its 21,400 inhabitants. In the Galilee there exist also Arab villages which inhabit more than 10,000 each, as Tamra – with 16,900 people, Merar – with 12,500, Sak hnin – with 16,800 and Arabe – with 12,500. Tamra and Sahknin, for instance, are close in their numbers of population to the Jewish town of Zefat which has 21,400 inhabitants. Nazareth, for instance, is bigger than any other Jewish town in the Central Galilee.

The minorities of Israel are concentrated mainly in two regions, in the Eron Valley and along the eastern part of the coastal plain. In each of them many thousands of minorities live in small towns and villages. The biggest Arab town in the Eron Valley is Um el–Fahem which totaled 26,200 inhabitants in 1991, and some other big villages there are Kara and Kafr Kara – with 9,500–9,600 inhabitants each. In the eastern coastal plain there are big Arab settlements as Baqa el–Garbiye – with 14,700 inhabitants, Tira – with 14,000 and Taybe with 21,200 inhabitants. The last two gained already the status of municipalities. These regional concentrations of minorities in Israel create two conspicuous phenomena: a definite regional majority of Arabs in the Central Galilee, and a dense Arab populated strip along the eastern coastal plain, parallel to the 'Green Line'. The minorities in Israel with their 914,200 people have ownership, right of posession and direct influence on the cultivation and exploitation of about 250,000 acres of land, or of about 10 percent of Israel's territory north to the Valley of Beer Sheba. Their villages are dispersed mainly between the Nazareth Mountains in the south and the Lebanon border in the north (Fig. 27).

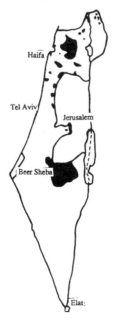

Fig. 27: Regions of Minorities in Israel

127

The minorities comprise, as mentioned, 18 percent of the total population of the country, and reside in 115 settlements. A quarter of them live in mixed Jewish–Arab towns as Jerusalem, Yafo, Lod, Ramla and Acre, a third – in the rural settlements in the Galilee, and the rest – in the Eron Valley and the eastern coastal plain. Besides them, there are about 70,000 Bedouins who live in the Negev and in the Judean Desert. The Arab population which resides along the eastern coastal plain, from Eron Valley in the north and the Modiin Region in the south, belonged once to a wider Arab region, and to a great triangle of space whose angular points were the towns of Nablus, Tulkarm and Jenin. A remainder of it belongs now to Israel's sovereign territory where about 100,000 Arabs live. In this area, as in other Arab villages of the Galilee, a regional homogenic system of services is developing along main communications axes, and around the big villages with 5,000 inhabitants and more. About two thirds of the rural Arab population is integrated in these regional systems which gradually are getting the form of isolated areas within the State of Israel.

The minority population increased very much since the establishment of the State of Israel. In 1948 they totaled not more than 156,000 people. Their increase in the 1970s and 1980s was about 4 percent per annum, one of the highest in the world. The birth rates among the Arabs decreased, but also the death rates, which makes the total increase still high. More than 75 percent of the Arabs in Israel were born after 1948. The Arab population does not have any trends to emigrate, they live in big families and are bounded to their lands.

The official governmental plan for population distribution toward the year 2000 envisages more than a million minorities in the country, and a big part of them – in settlements with more than 10,000 inhabitants each. The minorities are at present in a trend of economic and social change. While before 1948 their economy was based mainly on autarchic farms on small plots of land, after the establishment of the State their economical basis has considerable changed. Their agricultural occupation became integrated in the modern economy of Israel which increased their production, and followed by a higher standard of living. Because of their commercial connections with the urban markets in Israel, and their economic and social interrelations with the Israeli population, their traditional barriers of rural life were broken, more of them were occupied outside their villages, their occupation in agriculture declined, and more than a half of their manpower in the rural settlements is now occupied in non–agricultural branches. This change increased their income, but at the same time, also splitted their paternal homes into smaller families. The minorities' national aspiration increased their demands for new building sites, public institutions and pressure to convert agricultural land for housing. Lately, more industry has been initiated and developed in the Arab villages, which indicates first signs of semi–urbanization. The Israel government encouraged to a certain degree local government in the Arab sector, and some greater villages even received in the last years the status of towns.

Arabs and Jews

The difference in the geographical and demographic patterns of Arabs and Jews is one of the political, economic and social issues in Israel. The Jews in Israel have more economic priorities than the Arabs. Their advantages are higher in the dense populated Jewish areas of the central parts of the country. Their disadvantages lie mainly in the Arab populated areas of the Galilee and in the eastern coastal plain. The government tries to decrease these disadvantages with a policy of Jewish population distribution to these peripheral regions. The Arabs, on other hand, find advantage in being concentrated in certain regions of the country where they are able to encourage their sprawl of settlements and to seize open land for expansion, although the disadvantages of life in the periphery which decreases their opportunities for occupation, level of services and standard of living. In this aspect not much had been done by the Israeli authorities to advance the minorities' standard of living in the periphery. Regional and local planning has not been developed equally in the Jewish and Arab sectors, and created, therefore, differences in construction, housing, infrastructure, and building of roads, public institutions and industrial zones. The planning of the Arab village as a professional field is still backward, comparatively to urban and rural planning that exists in the Jewish sector. No clear conceptions regarding the immage and character of a rural Arab village exists yet, nor its special architectural features, and the new ways of construction that should be implemented. Not many planners and architects are engaged in the field of Arab village planning in cooperation with their inhabitants. Many villages lack with approved outline schemes, and modernization still did not reach all of them. Although rural planning is in a very advanced progress in many countries of the world, with interesting solutions to different kinds of rural population, in the Arab sector of Israel not much of it is implemented.

The Israeli government directs national and local development in the Arab sector in a slow motion. In the local level it aspires to improve housing, basic rural infrastructure and to diversify occupations, while in the national level it acts to prevent the Arabs to disperse their building on governmental–owned land, and that with a strong policy to keep a demographic balance between Jews and Arabs. The first level seems to be constructive, but it is connected with town planning restrictions in the villages, and with strict steps taken against deviations from the rules, despite that the density in the Arab villages is very high, and the economic and demographic pressure under which the population lives there, compells them in many cases to infringe the law and to change arable land into land for other uses.

The government's attitude to the minorities' situation does not supply enough solutions to the real problems they have. Although the government made efforts to improve development in the Arab sector, what still remained very conspicious is the Arab continuous struggle against confiscation of their lands in the Galilee for Jewish settlement, and also the Bedouins' struggle against the deployment from their pasture lands that they owned in the past. The Bedouins of the Negev were driven out from lands on which they lived for generations, and were replaced to some unsuccessfull settlements, east of Beer Sheba, where the government wanted to sedenterize them, although these settlements did not fit their ways of life.

One of the well–known expressions of the Arab population against the discrimination of their sector is ,the "Land Day" which is celebrated by them annually in mass–participation on March 31st, and which points out several facts: it symbolizes the minorities' identification with the Palestinians in the administrative territories under Israeli occupation; the deepening of national identity between the Arabs on both sides of the 'Green Line'; and the support they give to their local leaders who conduct the ways of struggle to achieve civil rights. The "Land Day" has a political meaning for the minorities, especially because of the existing 'Intifada', an uprise in the territories which has influenced their nationalistic emotions. It reveals the roots of the problems which the Arab have: land is for them a symbol and an essence. They relate to their land as to the origin of their existence, and the territory which enables them real holding in this country. They feel that they live on this land since ever, but with strong discrimination, without full civil rights, and with a low–ranking citizens' status. Their nationalistic aspirations are not less than these of the Palestinians in the territories, and the 'Green Line' which seperated between them in the past, did not make them better Israelis. While Israel does not demonstrate a clear minority policy, their future in the frame of the Jewish State remains blurred.

It should be mentioned, that the minorities in Israel created after years some irreversible basic facts, which may unsatisfy many Israeli politicians. 18 percent of Israel's population which owns hundreds of thousand acres of land is, to a certain degree, discriminated in planning and development; this population is getting urbanized very rapidly, does not emigrate, and needs a reasonable physical infrastructure for modern live; it advances in education, economy and social needs; it forms a nationalistic potential population which might not match with Israel's political aims; it is located adjacent to Israel's borders with the territories along the 'Green Line', with all the security problems which lie behind it.

130

In order to improve the whole situation of the minorities, it is needed to prepare for them in due time a national economic and settlement plan, according to their social characteristics; to develop a hierarchy of regional settlements with service centers of different size; to develop models of modern rural building; and to release to a certain degree agricultural land for housing, commerce and industry; and to advance in the bigger villages and semi-urban settlements the construction of public institutions, roads, industrial zones and parks.

After the gradual absorption of the Jewish mass immigration of the 1950s, and all the new towns which have been constructed for that purpose, time comes to convey financial sources to the Arab sector. Such a step may prevent further political tension in the area. There is still a danger, that the minorities in Israel, influenced by the Palestinians in the territories, may some time uprise and demand autonomy for themselves within the Israel's sovereign State, if further feelings of discrimination will not come to an end. The identification of the Arab minorities with the Palestinian's outburst of temper after the tragic massacre in the Cave of Machpela at Hebron in 1994, revealed the hidden wrath that exists among them against the government. One dramatic painful occurrence almost brought then to an Arab revolt against the army and the government, expressed by throwing stones on vehicles, mass–public demonstrations, tyre–burnings on highways and other sympthoms of anger, which were not known before. Their feelings of discrimination which lies under a thin cover of tolerancy, suddenly bursted out after the first fire spark that was liqhtened in Hebron.

Israel towards the 21st Century

The interest of mankind in what might happen in the 21st century is a world–wide phenomenon, mainly in developed countries. The beginning of a new century might also be seen as an intelectual and professional challenge for people, and especially for futurologists, who find interest in future occurrences. On one hand the 21st century creates productive imagination about possible different events which human society might experience, but on other hand, the next century is so near to come, that current events almost overhaul the future.

Israel is one of the developed countries in the world whose future is strongly interwoven in acts of innovation and creation. In this country, because of its small area and poor natural resources, national and regional planning of space for the future was always compulsive. Almost five decades of building and development have created in Israel innumerable facts in cities, in villages, in agriculture, in industry and in communications. The natural landscape has been changed continuously. The pressure of economic development grew from year to year, and the struggle on land–use became stronger. It is therfore worthwile to examine, from a geographical point of view, the spatial destinations of that country, its priorities of development, and the way it will shape its future toward the next century.

What is hidden in the future of the State of Israel? It may be assumed, that the country will be in future not much bigger than it was before the Six Day War in 1967. With perhaps some marginal additions, it will encompass an area of 25–30 thousand square kilometers, which is not very large for a country, and in these dimensions it will have to find solutions for the population increase and for the absorption of hundred of thousand of immigrants who may arrive. Natural increase plus immigration will result in the addition of a million people in the next decade. The State will have to provide dwellings for the growing population, and will do so in selected places in accordance with governmental guidelines for population distribution.

The population of Israel counted in 1995 about 5.3 million. Thus by the end of this century Israel will have almost Six million people. Such a large population will need a great deal of land for dwellings, economic activity and circulation. To scatter the population becomes harder every year, while the natural trend of people is towards crowding more and more, mainly in the coastal plain and in the areas which were historically the first settlement sites in the country. Although there will be some increased population in the Negev and in the Galilee, it must be recognized, that the coastal plain, where all fear overpopulation, will continue to absorb people, and become more densely populated. To maintain, for instance, a third of the population in the Tel Aviv conurbation, would mean two million people in the central parts of the country with a average density of 6,000 inhabitants per square kilometer.

Israel is a country where the pressure of urbanization on agricultural land is extremely high. The reason for that is that the country is very urbanized, with 89 per cent of its population living in cities or urban settlements; even the rates of natural increase and immigration to Israel are high; from Beer Sheba Valley northwards, and particular in the coastal plain, the population density is close to 500 inhabitants per square kilometer; the territory is small, the distances are short, most villages are close to cities, which naturally leads the pressure of urbanization on agricultural land.

Because of all that, in future no dispersed building of houses in cities will be possible, and no low–density housing will be allowed in neighbourhoods, because of deficiency of urban land potential. The 1950s development towns will have to reshape their urban and economic profile, their central business districts will be densed, and more multi–storey houses will be built where low–density zones were planned in the past. They will be populated by more inhabitants, get more services, commerce and industry, and will be better and more efficiently linked to the main communications arteries. Most of the urbanization will occur inside the big cities and conurbations, and also in outher urban fringe areas. The big cities will increase in their number of population, traffic load on the main roads will be higher, and more pressure will be imposed on the urban peripheries by the trend of establishing different kinds of suburbs. Even small–holders' (Moshavot) settlements will be more urbanized, and urban life in most of the Israeli settlements will be dominant.

The accessibility to the big cities will be more difficult, urban centers will be blocked because of the high rate of motorization which exists in the country, and the public will have to use more mass–transportation facilities, especially the inter–urban railway in Tel Aviv conurbation and the new railway lines which will be added in other parts of the country. It may be assumed, that the increase in the number of cars of 15 percent per annum will continue in the future as well. This means a persistent increase in private cars and an increasing burden on roads. The pressure of various transport needs in towns and outside them will continue, and it is doubtful, whether Israel will be able to cope with such an intensive development that characterises countries in advanced stages of development. It will be necessary to allot more land for parking, for widening roads and roundabouts, even at the cost of good land. Urban life will encourage the construction of more bridges, overpasses, underground passages and new communications means in the big cities. Israel has not yet reached a saturation point in private cars, so that it can look forward to several years of increasing ownership and the development of the necessary facilities at the expence of the little land available. Economic development is inconceivable without transport developments, so that clash with other vital uses is inevitable unless unused land is sacrified for this function. The building of houses will be executed in a modern style which might lead, after many years of experience to an original architectural style in housing. The three urban concentrations of Tel Aviv, Haifa and Jerusalem and their environs will continue to grow and constitute greater attractivity than other places in the country, so that for the governmental policy of population distribution it will become more difficult to prevent these trends.

It may be expected that new kinds of non–agricultural settlements will be created all over the country. Among them will be the industrial village, which is a rural cooperative unit, whose main source of livelihood will be not agriculture but rather industry and services; the community–type settlement, which in its final stage will contain 200–300 families, enjoying great independence, despite the cooperative of which all residents are members. In this form of settlement the economic system will be based on independent family units joined together, whose employment and means of production will be within the settlement; the topsite settlement as a political means of hastening the solution of the problems of settling the Galilee, may also be developed intensively. Such a settlement is new in its means, but very similar to its 'tower and stockage' predessors in its principles. The topsites may solve the problem of holding the land, but it is doubtful whether they can change the demographic balance in the Galilee; the inanimate center as an inhabited complex, located between villages whose function is to supply educational, public, personal and other services and employment in industry and crafts, may also be a solution in low–dense areas; and the exurb as an open settlement of rural character, serving mainly as a residential quarter for a larger urban concentration, will be another new form of settlement. The population in an exurb is likely to range between 500 to 2,000 families, so that local services of a reasonable standard can be provided, and a decent social fabric evolved. Construction will be on land purchased by the residents.

It seems, that the approach to economic development in future will not be routine. It will be necessary to exploit the talent of the many Russian–Jewish immigrants who arrived to Israel since 1989, and to encourage high–tec industry in the fields of technology, medicine, biology and aviation. Lack of soil and water will bring to radical changes in agricultural production, in irrigation systems, in developing early–fruit plantations on conveyed soil to sandy areas, in the adjustment of new species to mountainous and arid climates, and irrigation with re–used or low–salty water will be extended. The rural population will be more urbanized in their needs and ways of life, in occupation, services and in consumption.

Industry will also be widened by improving the ways of production and the level of manufacturing. Deficiency in basic raw materials will bring to the development of light industrial branches in which the needed rate of raw material is low. The electronic and sophisticated branches demonstrate already nowadays the first stages of such a process.

In the coastal plain the population will increase very fast, and although the existing governmental trends of population dispersal, there will be no escape from a dense populated coastal plain between Hadera in the north and Ashqelon in the south. Tel Aviv's extended circle and area of urban influence, reaching the Yarqon River to the north, Holon and Bat Yam to the south, and Ramat Gan and Bene Beraq to the east, will approach Netanya to the north, Rehovot to the south and Petah Tiqwa to the east. Live quality in the Tel Aviv metropolitan area will not be much better in the future, and may be similar to that which exists in other big cities of the world. People will suffer there from air pollution and noise, the consciousness to the quality of environment will be greater among people and will also be more demonstrated in different platforms of political parties. The intensity with which agricultural land will be transformed for other uses will spread radially, as the urban demands of the cities will grow. In the wake of the continual dwindling of the land reserves for residential purposes for industrial plants, and other uses in the large cities, there will be a tendency to convert agricultural land in medium–sized and smaller tows as well, which include 40–50 percent of the areas in the country.

A new national crossroad will be constructed in the next years between Beer Sheba in the south and the Galilee in the north, about 230 kilometers long. Lateral roads in the Tel Aviv area and along the coastal plain will be connected with this new highway and encourage the transfer of more commercial and economic activity to the eastern part of the plain, which has suffered for many years from lack of development.

Changes may also occur in regional development. The spatial metropolitan rings around Tel Aviv will be filled with inhabitants as a result of the Russian–Jewish immigration which began in the 1990s, and the concentration of many new economic projects in the central coastal plain. Ashdod in the south, Lod, Ramla and the new town of Modiin in the east and Netanya in the north, will be the new borderlines of the intensive urban sprawl which will take place along the coastal plain.

At the beginning of the next decade there will be at least one million–town in the country, apparently Jerusalem, although its existing political and delicate situation. Tel Aviv will be the second, and Haifa – the third. The city of Jerusalem will strive to keep its urban unity, and may perhaps conduct a new system of municipal administration in the form of a super–municipality for its two peoples, the Jews and the Arabs. The Jewish–Orthodox population in Jerusalem will increase, more educational and cultural institutions will be built in the city, and the position of Jerusalem as a capital will be strenghtened, whether as a pilgrimage city or as the most important touristic site. Because of political restrictions in the north, east and south, the city will expand mainly to the western mountainous 'Corridor', while the Arab population in East Jerusalem will increase their rural periphery and dense it by newcomers and commuters.

Haifa will be the third largest city in Israel, after Jerusalem and Tel Aviv, and will compete economically and socially with cities located in the coastal plain, and especially with Ashdod, where the second biggest harbour of the country has been built. Haifa's main increase will probably occur as being the capital of the Galilee, with a large periphery of villages and suburbs that exist around. Along the Zebulun Valley, between Haifa and Acre, an industrial agglomeration will develop, as a counter–weight to Haifa's own economy.

The Galilee and the Negev are the two regions for Israel's potential development in the future. Both will compete for their national position in drawing investments, while both have as development regions priorities and deficiencies. The priority of the Galilee lies in its proportional higher population, in its potential existing manpower, in convenient climate, diverse landscape, resources of water and its proximity to Haifa. Its deficiency lies in its high topography and in its proportional large rural Arab population. In any case, the Galilee will be in future a demographic arena where Jews and Arabs will try to diverse the existing demographic equilibrium in favour of each side. Another expected trend will be recognized in the Galilee, and that will be the Bedouin sprawl from their periodically concentrations to semi–established sub–villages which may in time achieve official status as settlements.

The priority of the Negev lies in its wide empty space, but its main deficiencies lie in its remoteness from the economic center of the country, its sparse populated areas, its arid climate and its scarcity of water. May be, that as a result of these compared conditions, the Galilee will gain more investment in the future, mainly in light industries and infrastructure which will enable many settlements and topsites to develop, while the Negev will obtain mainly heavy industries which need large space, as chemical factories and installations which threaten to pollute their surroundings. Most of the development in the Negev will occur around Beer Sheba. The railway line to Elat will be completed, and the city of Elat will become in future the main tourist center in the south, together with a combined operation with the Jordanian city of Aqaba.

Land in Israel will be also needed for purposes other than settlements, population and transport. There is no doubt, that the rising standard of living will be reflected in a demand for recreational areas, suburban dwellings, public institutions, parks, nature reserves, bathing beaches etc. As the population has not yet reached the saturation point in affluence and standard of living, there will be a demand for land for these purposes. The construction of power stations, for instance, will be one of the great consumers of land. As to industry, even greater industrialization is to be expected. Most of the industrial zones in the populated settlements are fillinq up. There is little reserve land for this purpose in the big cities but, as said, more in the Negev and Galilee. However, because of the economic advantages of the coastal plain, industry will prefer to locate there, and create pressures on land–use of an intensity herefore unknown. Industry is gradually emerging into the inter–city areas, and causing a significant loss of agricultural land. It will be difficult to counter the industrialists when they prove that their contribution to the economy is considerable, greater than that of agriculture. Faced with demand for land for such important uses as dwellings, population, transport, industry, recreation, and energy in the future, the question remains whether Israel will have enough land for all that.

As regards possibilities for land development, Israel will be in no better situation in the next decade. To the extent that the needs of building, transport, industry, energy and recreation can be adapted to the objective situation of the land potential, and to the extent that the sectorial demands for land can be restrained, Israel will be able to more or less preserve the condition that prevails at present, and that is the reasonable optimum. If that will not be done, and Israel will succumb to various pressures, agricultural land to other uses, it shall gradually loose the land basis on which the State was established, and it will return into a country of concrete, accessories.

Bibliography

Abbu–Ayyash A. (1981), "Israeli Planning Policy in the Occupied Territories", Journal of Palestinian Studies 11, 1. pp. 111–123.

Allon Y. (1976), "The Case for Defensible Borders", Foreign Affairs, 55 (1), pp. 38–53.

Benvenisti M. and *5. Khayat* (eds.) (1988), "The West Bank and Gaza Atlas", The West Bank Data Base Project, The Jerusalem Post, Jerusalem, 140 pp.

Benvenisti M. (1984), "West Bank Data Base Project, A Survey of Israel's Policies", American Enterprise Institute, Studies in Foreign Policy, Washington.

Benvenisti M. (1983), "Jerusalem Study of a Polarized Community, Research Paper 3, Jerusalem.

Brutzkus E. (1970), "Regional Policy in Israel", Ministry of the Interior, Jerusalem, pp. 42–44.

Brutzkus E. (1969), "Regional Policy in Israel", Report submitted to the 1969 Annual Conference of Permanent Committee for Regional Planning, Jerusalem, 50 pp.

Central Bureau of Statistics (1994), "Statistical Annual", 44, Jerusalem.

Central Bureau of Statistics (1988), "Immigration to Israel 1988", Special Series, 858, Table 6, Jerusalem.

Central Bureau of Statistics (1983), "Population Census 1983", Jerusalem.

Costa F.J. and A.G. Noble (1988), "Planning Arab Towns", Geographical Review, vol. 76, pp. 160–172.

Dash Y. and E. Efrat (1964), "The Israel Physical Master Plan", Ministry of the Interior, Jerusalem.

Dash J. et al. (1964), "National Planning for the Redistribution of Population and Establishment of New Towns in Israel", Ministry of the Interior, Jerusalem.

Efrat E. (1994), "Jewish Settlement in the West Bank: Past, Present and Future", Israel Affairs, England, vol. 1, No. 1, pp. 135–148.

Efrat E. (1994a), "The New Development Towns of Israel (1948–1993)" – a Reappraisal", Cities, Vol. 11, No. 4, pp. 247-252.

Efrat E. (1992), "Toward the Giving–Up of Territories", 'Haaretz' Newspaper, Tel Aviv, 16 August, (Hebrew).

Efrat E. (1992a), "Peace Patterns in the Insurgency Region of Judea and Samaria", Small Wars & Insurgencies, Frank Cass, London, vol. 3, No. 3, pp. 257–271.

Efrat E. (1990), "The Geography of Direct Absorption of Soviet–Jewish Immigrants", in: Geography of Absorption (A. Gonen ed.), The Israel Geographical Society and the Department of Geography, Jerusalem, pp. 75–88 (Hebrew).

Efrat E. (1989), "The New Towns of Israel (1948–1988) – a Reappraisal, Minerva Publication, Nunich, 184 pp.

Efrat E. (1988), "Geography and Politics in Israel since 1967", Frank Cass, London, 225 pp.

137

Efrat E. and A. G. Noble (1988), "Problems of Reunified Jerusalem", Cities, The International Quarterly of Urban Policy, vol. 5, No. 4, pp. 326–343.

Efrat E. (1982), "Spatial Patterns of Jewish and Arab Settlements in Judea and Samaria", in: D. J. Elazar (ed.),

Judea, Samaria and Gaza: Views on the Present and Future', American Enterprise, Institute for Public Policy Research, Washington, pp. 9–43.

Elazar D. J. (1982), "Judea, Samaria and Gaza: Views on the Present and Future", American Enterprise Institute, Studies in Foreign Policy, Washington, 22 pp.

Falah G. (1989), "Israeli 'Judaization' Policy in Galilee and its Impact on Local Arab Urbanization", Political Geography Quarterly, vol. 8, No. 3, pp. 229–253.

Falah G. (1985), "Recent Jewish Colonization in Hebron", in: D. Newman (ed.), 'The Impact of Gush Emunim', Croom Helm, London.

Finkel R. and J. Margulis (1991), "The Potential to Absorb New Immigrants in Rural Settlements and in Peripheral Areas", Development Study Center, Rehovot, Israel, 119 pp. (Hebrew).

Goodman H. (1974), "Jerusalem as the Capital of Israel", in: 'Jerusalem' (J.N. Oesterreicher and A. Sinai eds.), John Day, pp. 129–130.

Gradus Y. (1983), "The Role of Politics in Regional Inequality: The Israel Case", Annals of Association of American Geographers, 73, pp. 388–403.

Grossman D. (1992), "Rural Process–Pattern Relationship", Praeger, 213 pp.

Grossman D. and Z. Safrai (1980), "Settlements in Western Samaria", Geographical Review, 70, pp. 446–461.

Harris W. W. (1980), "Taking Root: Israeli Settlement in the West Bank, Golan, Gaza and Sinai", John Wiley, New York.

Harris W. W. (1978), "War and Settlement Change: the Golan Heights and the Jordan Rift 1967–1977", Transactions of the Institute of British Geographers, 3, pp. 309–330.

Jewish Agency (1990), "Report to the Assembly of the Jewish Agency, The Department for Immigration and Absorption, Jerusalem, p.7.

Kahan D. (1983), "Agriculture and Water in the West Bank and Gaza", West Bank Data Base Project, Jerusalem.

Katz Y. (1992), "Jewish Settlement in the Hebron Mountains and the Etzion Bloc", Bar–Ilan University, Ramat Gan, Israel, 304 pp. (Hebrew).

Kellerman A. (193), "Settlement Frontiers Revisited: The Case of Israel and the West Bank", Tijdschrift voor Economische en Sociale Geografie, 84, 1, pp. 27–39.

Lustik I. (1981), "Israel and the West Bank after Alon Moreh: the Mechanics of defacto Annexation", Middle East Journal, 39, 4, pp. 557–577.

McCall R.W. (1969), "Insurgent State: Territorial Bases of Revolution", Annals of Association of American Geographers, vol. 59, pp. 632–641.

Ministry of Absorption (1991), "Report on Immigration between 1.1.1990–31.12.1990", Statistical Data, Jerusalem.

Ministry of Absorption (1990), "Report on Immigration between 1.1.1989–31.12.1989", Statistical Data, Jerusalem.

Newman D. (1994), "Towards Peace in the Middle East: the Formation of State Territiories in Israel, the West Bank and the Gaza Strip", Geography, pp. 263–268.

Newman D. (ed.) (1985), "The Impact of Gush Emunim", Croom Helm, London.

Newman D. (1985), "The Evolution of Political Landscape: Geographical and Territorial Implication of Jewish Colonization in the West Bank", Middle Eastern Studies, 21, 2, pp. 195–205.

Newman D. (1984), "The Development of the Yishuv Kehillati in Judea and Samaria, Political Process and Settlement Forms", Tijdschrift voor Economische en Sociale Geographie, 75, 2, pp. 140–150.

Newman D. (1984), "Ideological and Political Influences of Israeli Rurban Colonization: The West Bank and Galilee Mountains", Canadian Geographer, 28, (2), pp. 142–155.

Newman D. (1982). "Jewish Settlement in the West Bank: The Role of Gush Emunim", Occasional Paper, 16, Centre of Middle Eastern Studies, Univ. of Durham, U.K.

Noble A.G. and E. Efrat (1990), "Geography of the Intifada", Geographical Review, vol. 80, No. 3, pp. 287–307.

Portugali J. (1991), "Jewish Settlement in the Occupied Territories, Israel's Settlement Structure and the Palestinians", Political Geography Quarterly, 10, 1, pp. 26–53.

Portugali J. (1988), "Nationalism, Social Theory and the Israeli/Palestinian Case", in: Nationalism, Self Determination and Geography (R. J. Johnston, D. Knight and E. Kofman eds.), Croom Helm, London, pp. 151–165.

Rokach A. (1982), "The Galilee Development and Settlement", The Jewish Agency, Department of Rural Settlement, Jerusalem.

Romann N. and A. Weingrod (1992), "Living Together Seperately – Arabs and Jews in Contemporary Jerusalem", Princeton University Press, N. J., 258 pp.

Romann M. (1986), "Jewish Kiryat Arba and Arab Hebron", West Bank Data Base Project, Jerusalem.

Romann M. (1981), "Interrelations between Jewish and Arab Sectors in Jerusalem", The Jerusalem Institute for Israeli Studies, vol. 11, pp. 9–10 (Hebrew).

Romann N. (1978), "Jerusalem since 1967: a Profile of a Reunited City", GeoJournal, 6, 2, pp. 499–506.

Rumly D. and Y. Oren (1993), "The Political Geography of the Control of the Minorities", Tijdschrift voor Economische en Sociale Geographie, 84, 1, pp. 51–64.

Sabbagh J. (1994), "Jüdisch–Arabische Interaktionen im Jerusalemer Stadtkern", Mainzer Geographische Studien, Heft 40, pp. 1667–178.

Sharon A. (1966), "Planning Jerusalem, the Old City and its Environs", Weidenfeld and Nicolson, Jerusalem.

Spiegel E. (1966), "The New Towns in Israel" Karl Kraemer Verlag, Stuttgart/Bern, 192 pp.

Wolf A. T. (1995), "Hydropolitics along the Jordan River", United Nations University Press, N.Y., 272 pp.

(1984), "The Allon Plan", Efal, 14 pp. (Hebrew).

About the Author

Prof. Elisha Efrat studied at the Hebrew University of Jerusalem, concentrating on geography, Planning and Statistics, being awarded a B.A. in 1955, MA. in 1957, and Ph.D. in 1963. Since 1967 he has lectured on geography at Tel Aviv University, being appointed Senior Lecturer (1968), Associate Professor in Applied Geography (1972), and Full Professor in Geography (1983). He has written many articles on political, planning, development and urban subjects in Israel. His books include: "The Israel Physical Master Plan" (with J. Dash) (1964); "Jerusalem and the Corridor" (1967); "Geoqraphy in Israel" (with E. Orni) (1971); "Israel towards the Year 2000" (1978); "Elements of Urban Geography" (1979); "Settlement Geography of Israel" (1981); "Urbanization in Israel" (1984); "Geography and Politics in Israel" (1988); "The New Towns of Israel 1948-1988 - a Reappraisal" (1989); and "Rural Geography of Israel" (1994).

Mobilität und Normenwandel

Changing Norms and Mobility

Band 8

Pokol, Béla:

Komplexe Gesellschaft. Eine der möglichen Luhmannschen Soziologien

1990, 271 Seiten, ISBN 3-88339-823-3 kart. 49,80 DM

Band 9

Gunlicks, Arthur B. / Voigt, Rüdiger (Hrsg.):

Förderalismus in der Bewährungsprobe: Die Bundesrepublik in den 90er Jahren

1991, 281 Seiten, ISBN 3-88339-919-1, 2. Auflage 1994 kart. 49,80 DM

Band 10

Briesen, Detlef / Gans, Rüdiger / Flender, Armin:

Regionalbewußtsein in Montanregionen im 19. und 20. Jahrhundert: Saarland – Siegerland – Ruhrgebiet

1994, 206 Seiten, ISBN 3-8196-0209-7 kart. 34,80 DM

Band 11

Mielke, Gerd / Edith, Ulrich:

Honoratioren oder Parteisoldaten?

1994, 148 Seiten, ISBN 3-8196-0210-0 kart. 24,80 DM

Band 12

Scherer, Roland:

Der Einfluß der Regionalplanung auf die kommunale Bauleitplanung

1994, 162 Seiten, ISBN 3-8196-0208-9 kart. 29,80 DM

Band 13

Gabriel, Oscar W. und Voigt, Rüdiger (Hrsg.):

Kommunalwissenschaftliche Analysen

1994, 328 Seiten, ISBN 3-8196-0262-3 kart. 49,80 DM

Band 14

Frevel, Bernhard:

Kleines Studienbuch. Politische Soziologie / Politikwissenschaft

1995, 188 Seiten, ISBN 3-8196-0342-5 kart. 29,80 DM